A Modern System of Pass Defense

JERICHO:

JERICHO:

A Modern System

of

Pass Defense

DEWAYNE "DEWEY" KING

Backfield Coach

Rutgers—The State University

Prentice-Hall, Inc., Englewood Cliffs, N. J.

JERICHO: A Modern System of Pass Defense, by DeWayne "Dewey" King
© 1963 by Prentice-Hall, Inc., Englewood Cliffs, N. J.

Library of Congress Catalog Card Number 63-14027

PRINTED IN THE UNITED STATES OF AMERICA
50936—BC

GOD has surrounded me with a Christian, sports-loving family. The Bible and athletics have always enjoyed a remarkable coexistence in our home.

This book is humbly dedicated to my family: my wife, *Peggy*, and young son, *Douglas DeWayne*; my parents, *Mr. and Mrs. A. R. King*, and my three brothers—*Ronald*, *Louis* and *Harold*.

Each one has given me so much. I am in their debt and shall always be grateful to them for their deep and abiding love.

—DeWayne "Dewey" King

"TO me, the coaching profession is one of the noblest and most far-reaching in building manhood. No man is too good to be the athletic coach for youth. Not to drink, not to gamble, not to smoke, not to swear . . . to be fair-minded . . . to deal justly . . . to be honest in thinking and square in dealing . . . not to bear personal malice or harbor hatred against rivals . . . not to be swell-headed in victory or over-alibi in defeat . . . to be the sportsman and gentleman at all times . . . those should be the ideals of the coach."

—Amos Alonzo Stagg

CERVANTES didn't know anything about football, but that didn't stop him from coming up with a lot of good lines, some of which are still being quoted after 400 years. One of his homely adages declares that "The proof of the pudding is in the eating."

This always seemed reasonable to me, as it might to anybody who likes puddings, so when I heard that Dewey King was writing a book on pass defense I was eager to read it. For if Cervantes was right, this was a book worth reading. All I could think of was the undefeated, untied Rutgers team of 1961, and there was the pudding, with the proof neatly wrapped up in it.

Those Rutgers boys of 1961 did more damage with forward passes other people threw against them than any team I ever saw. Pass defense, as taught by King, became practically another arm of the Rutgers attack. It became a game within a game. In fact, after King's *Scarlet* pupils had intercepted five passes and turned three of them into touchdowns to beat Colgate, an enemy quarterback had to be psychopathic to throw against them at all.

Another reason I looked forward to this book was that pass defense always has ranked high among the mysteries of football to me. Since I guess I am of an inquisitive nature, I thought there was a chance here to learn more about it. And there was.

When I read the book I found that King had made pass defense exactly what it looked like as Rutgers played it—a separate game and an attacking weapon. Dewey believes in defense so strongly, and teaches it so well, that I found he expects his boys to intercept one pass in every eight thrown. Better still, he gets his boys to expect the same thing.

This success in instilling confidence, in getting his boys to think and believe as he does, is the hallmark of a good teacher. Pass defense, many coaches have told me, is the hardest single department of football to teach and to learn. So, when you have a coach who can teach it superlatively well, the fellow is practically worth his weight in 50-yard line tickets.

Dewey's success in coaching pass defense probably stems from two things—his insistence on definiteness and his flair for the psychological.

Starting from the very practical approach that rushing the passer is the best defense there is, King quickly gets over to the covering of receivers. Here he immediately takes the positive, definite track by stating this preference for man-for-man coverage rather than zone. Man-for-man is not the final answer to all pass defense by any means, but one of its great values is that it is definite. Every defensive back knows exactly whom he is covering. Guessing is reduced to a minimum.

On the psychological side King builds on the basic idea that pass defense is both important and difficult and that it takes a good man to play in the exclusive company of a good defensive secondary. This pride is aroused and a sense of teamwork and reliance of one boy on another is instilled.

King also teaches an aggressive pass defense, hammering home the idea that the instant the enemy turns the ball loose, it is a possible touchdown for his boys. He takes pains to point out that there are five ways for the defense to score, as against only three for the offense.

Exemplifying this aggressive attitude are the stars King has pasted on the helmets of his backs, one for each interception. This, of course, is part of the psychological approach too. The boys take pride in winning the stars. And the stars exert a warning and restraining effect on the enemy quarterbacks. They are going to think twice before they throw the ball anywhere near a Rutgers back with three or four stars on his helmet.

But perhaps the single thing for which King will be best remembered, is the word that he has given to football—"Jericho!"

This is the shout a boy gives when he intercepts a pass, to inform his teammates that the ball is theirs and that they are to knock down enemy tacklers with all possible dispatch.

Many interception words have been used by coaches over the years—"Geronimo," "Block," "Oskie," etc. But none is as sharp, as penetrating, as galvanizing, as "Jericho!" The word has become so rooted in the minds of King's boys that they no longer even refer to an interception as an interception. They call it a Jericho.

If as a coach you don't get some very worthwhile ideas from this book and, if you are a fan, you don't derive a better understanding of pass defense, you'd better turn to tennis!

Len Elliott, Sports Editor
Newark (N.J.) Evening News

Preface

PASS defense is a much-discussed subject among football coaches. There are many ideas and concepts regarding the subject, dealing with the theory, type, philosophy and methods of teaching. It is a challenging and extraordinarily frustrating phase of football to teach. Personally, I enjoy coaching pass defense and have received a tremendous amount of satisfaction from the results of our work—but teaching pass defense is one challenge and writing about it is yet another.

I approach the writing of this book with a deep sense of humility; yet with strong convictions about the basic concept of pass defense. This includes our theory of over-all team defense, philosophy of pass defense, the psychological factors so deeply involved in it, the basic principles we teach, our three-deep and four-deep coverage, and my thoughts regarding the teaching of pass defense, along with the drills we use. All these phases will be discussed in this book.

I welcome the opportunity to share my ideas and beliefs about this controversial subject. I am not selling my particular theories and methods. This is what I believe, this is the way we do it and it has been successful. As a result, I believe in it

13

one hundred percent. Our boys share my convictions. This is all-important and the *real* reason why the pass defense has been successful.

My thoughts on this subject are offered with the hope that some one thing or some part of these beliefs will be of aid to a fellow coach who takes pride in coaching pass defense.

The following record achieved by our 1961 undefeated Rutgers football team serves to strengthen my convictions regarding our theory of pass defense.

Rutgers intercepted 23 passes, returned them for 405 yards (17.6 yards average per interception) and 4 touchdowns. We led the nation in this category. Safetyman Sam Mudie pilfered 6 enemy aerials (4th nationally), returned them for 167 yards (1st nationally) and 2 touchdowns. Our opponents completed 63 passes of 151 for 884 yards and 5 touchdowns, (98.2 yards per game average). Our 405 yards gained on returned interceptions subtracted from their 884 yards gained on forward passes gives them a net passing total of 479 yards. This is an average of 53.2 yards gained per game, via passing. We intercepted 1 of every 6.5 passes thrown at us and had a 15.2 interception percentage; which was number one in the nation for 1961. Another point of interest concerning our pass defense: our opponents scored 5 touchdowns by passing. We returned 4 intercepted passes for touchdowns; which gave the opponents a net total of 1 touchdown, via passing, in 9 games.

Our opponents, on two point plays, attempted 11 passes. They completed 3, we intercepted 2 (Mudie and Yaksick); which gave us a grand total of 25 for the 1961 season.

Sam Mudie	7**	Bill Herring	1
Bob Yaksick	4	Bill Speranza	1*
Pierce Frauenheim	4*	Joe Kowalski	1
Keith Krayer	3	Dwain Painter	1
Jon Paulson	2	Tom Kocaj	1

* Denotes interception returned for a touchdown.

I trust that my deep-rooted feelings concerning the challenge of teaching pass defense, my convictions regarding theory, the sense of pride and satisfaction that I have concerning the accomplishments of our pass defense, will stimulate and challenge your thinking as you read this book.

In Acknowledgment

Our pass defense, just as football itself, has evolved through the years to what we are teaching today. From its beginnings to the present, there have been many boys who have helped make it effective. I have learned from these young men and would be remiss if I did not mention some of the backfield men, who throughout my 14-year coaching career, have made significant contributions to the success of the pass defense. Sam Parks at McKinley High School, Canton, Ohio, was such a man. Gary Lowe and Earl Morrall, as freshmen at Michigan State, displayed a natural adeptness for pass defense. During our stay at the University of Pennsylvania such young men as Francis Riepl, Richard Ross, Richard Koze, Fred Doelling, and John Terpak contributed immeasurably to the success of the pass defense.

Other outstanding defensive performers were John Hanlon, David Coffin, Peter Schantz, and George Koval. These boys collaborated to lead the Ivy League in the field of pass interceptions for three years.

Pass Defenders Also Outstanding on Offense

Pass defense is just one segment in the over-all development of a good football team. This is shown clearly by the fact that most of these boys were outstanding offensive players, too. Riepl, starting his first college game as a sophomore in 1955, against Notre Dame, returned the opening kick-off 108 yards for a touchdown. Fred Doelling gained 1,568 yards in his three-year career to become the leading ground-gainer in Pennsylvania football history and was named All-East halfback in 1959. Koval was the greatest passer I have ever coached. He threw 17 touchdown passes during his three-year college grid career. Hanlon and Coffin were fine runners with speed, power and durability. Both developed into outstanding blockers while playing for the "Red and Blue."

At Rutgers I have had the good fortune to coach several outstanding pass defenders. During the 1961 season Rutgers led the nation in pass interceptions. The boys particularly responsible for this enviable record were: Pierce Frauenheim, Robert Yaksick, Samuel Mudie, and Joseph Kowalski (the finest linebacker I have coached). Other players, such as William Speranza, Keith Krayer, Robert Harrison, All-American center Alex Kroll, Thomas

Kocaj, Jon Paulson, and Steve Simms, All-East full-back in 1961, also made valuable contributions. Any list of outstanding pass defense men must also include Arnold Byrd and Paul Strelick who played for us in 1960 and 1962 respectively. I am grateful to all these boys and to many others, who go nameless, who have helped make our pass defense successful through the years.

While these athletes by their performance on the football field helped make this book possible, the man who helped me considerably during the actual writing of the manuscript was John F. McDonald, Assistant Director of Public Relations at Rutgers University. He read the manuscript, chapter by chapter, as it was written and made many helpful, succinct suggestions. I am deeply grateful to him for his help throughout the preparation of this book. A word of gratitude also goes to Mrs. George Lambert and Mrs. Monroe Pray who typed the manuscript.

No man is an island—everyone is affected and influenced by the people around us. Particularly is this true regarding those we work for and within our professions. We are affected to a greater or lesser degree, depending upon the existing circumstances at the time. I know that each coach I have served with or under has given me something, be it large or small.

It has been my good fortune to work for such outstanding head coaches as Richard Miller, at my *alma mater*, the University of North Dakota; Clarence L. "Biggie" Munn at Michigan State University; Steve Sebo at the University of Pennsylvania; and now Dr. John F. Bateman at Rutgers

University. In addition to these head coaches, I have worked with such fine assistant coaches, many of them now head coaches, as Frank Zazula at North Dakota; Duffy Daugherty; Earle Edwards; Dan Devine; Robert Devaney; Don Mason, and John Kobs. At the University of Pennsylvania our staff included C. A. "Tim" Temerario, to whom I owe so much; Paul Riblett; George Terlep; John Butler; Bernie Lemonick; Robert Graham, and the aforementioned John Bateman. Fellow staff members here at Rutgers are Matthew Bolger, Warren Schmakel, Frank Burns, and Robert Naso. These men comprise one of the finest staffs with which I have been associated.

Every one of these men has influenced me—but the man and coach who had the greatest impact on my life and affected me most is a man whom I have never met—AMOS ALONZO STAGG. This man is recognized not only as a great football coach but also as a strong, vibrant Christian. His life, both in word and deed, is a challenge to all of us who come after him in the football coaching profession. It is my conviction that *he is the greatest man American football has produced.* His marvelous coaching record and dynamic Christian life combine to make him, in my opinion, without peer in our country's list of great coaches. He never drank liquor nor smoked tobacco and did not use profanity. His influence on the young men he coached, over a 72-year coaching career, surpasses comprehension.

His winning coaching record alone would rank him with the greats in the coaching profession—but what makes him truly remarkable and lifts him above the level of other giants in our profession is that his name has always stood for character of the highest degree, rugged honesty, and stern simplicity, in addition to many other fine attributes. Everything in his personality and character has always been intolerant of the cheap and tawdry. Never would he advocate or allow compromise with Christian standards or convictions to secure a momentary triumph, either on or off the athletic field.

Coach Stagg, by combining his marvelously inventive mind and unique coaching skills with his inherent and unwavering Christian ideals, truly is *the grand old man of American football.* Others have called Amos Alonzo Stagg the "All-time Christian coach" and a "minister on the field"; his coaching creed is reprinted in the front of this book.

I am grateful that such a man was directed by God into football. It is to the glory of American football that his name will forever be associated with the game. His life is a challenge and inspiration to me. Only through the medium of personal correspondence have I met this great man, but he is the person I have chosen to emulate in dedicating my life to being a Christian football coach.

Contents

21

3. Psychological Factors in Pass Defense, 69

4. Ten Basic Principles of Our Pass Defense, 81

5. Three-Deep Pass Defense Coverage, 101

Contents

6. Four-Deep Pass Defense Coverage, 127

Contents

7. Teaching Pass Defense in Early Season Practice, 163

8. Practicing Pass Defense During the Season, 175

Contents

Contents

List
of Illustrations

Philosophy

of Over-All

Team *Defense*

Chapter One

PASS defense is the subject of this book. However before concentrating on this controversial subject, it is necessary to set forth the philosophy of total team defense used at *Rutgers*. This will give the reader a better understanding of our total defensive plan, of which pass defense is a vital part.

We Use Multiple Defense—and Play Percentages

We are strong believers in the theory of multiple defense. We do not feel that any one defense can stop all the opponents' good plays and passes. There is no single, satisfactory, all-purpose defense in modern football. Multiple defense is the answer to this problem—but it must be used in its entirety and not limited to one or two alignments and games. It becomes an all-purpose defense only when all facets of it are employed in a knowledgeable manner.

Principles That Constitute Multiple Defense

Multiple defense is based on four basic principles:

1. We line up in three different alignments.
2. From the three alignments the linemen execute games.
3. Pass defense men have three types of coverage.
4. We play percentages.

All sound defense is based on:

- Good stance
- Movement on movement of the ball
- Controlling the offensive man
- Reaction to the ball
- Effective release
- Good pursuit
- Vigorous tackling

Good multiple defense also includes all these qualities—but in addition it possesses several points that make it unique and consequently set it apart from other defensive ideologies. These qualities are:

1. When a lineman has a game to execute he goes to his point of responsibility—then reacts to the ball. We get movement from our defensive men.
2. We play percentages all the way. A specific play or pass against a particular alignment or game may hurt us—but the next time that same play or pass is run, it may lose yardage or be intercepted.
3. Multiple defense is designed to bend but not break. Remembering the point just discussed and also the fact that multiple defense must be called and used in a knowledgeable manner gives this theory of defense an elasticity that most others do not possess. We will bend but not break.

The four principles of multiple defense are discussed in the ensuing paragraphs.

Philosophy of Over-All Team Defense

1. We line up in three different alignments:

   a. A 5-3 alignment that is called a 53 (Figure 1).
   b. A 5-4 alignment that is called a 54 (Figure 2).
   c. A 6-1 alignment that is called a 61 (Figure 3).

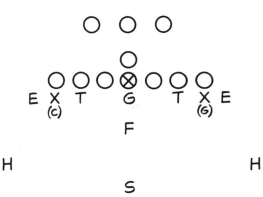

Figure 1: 53 Alignment

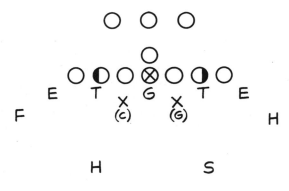

Figure 2: 54 Alignment

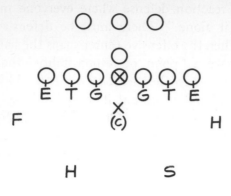

Figure 3: 61 Alignment

Our men are placed in these alignments by the first unit of a simple three-unit numbering system. Our defensive signals are called this way:

 53 Basic Special
 54 Pinch Box
 61 Out Box-Set

The number denotes the alignment, the middle word identifies the game, and the third word is the pass defense coverage.

It is imperative, when using multiple defense, to operate as a unit. Individual glory must be foregone for the benefit and betterment of the team. There can be no heroes. Everyone on defense must have faith that each person will carry out his assignment in the defense that has been called.

There can be no "free-lancing" or compensating. These are team defenses devised for eleven men to execute specific assignments simultaneously and in a synchronized manner. Multiple defense is not

   Philosophy of Over-All Team Defense

an individual reaction defense where everyone involved "goes it alone." There must be defensive discipline. When the offensive center snaps the ball all linemen have a "point of responsibility" that they must go to—*then* they react to the ball. This is sometimes difficult to do but it must be done if the defense is to be effective. Otherwise it will be rendered totally ineffective.

The players must believe in multiple defense and have faith in each other. When these two factors are realized, the defense will be successful.

2. From the three alignments linemen execute games.

Multiple defense is devised to provide the defensive men with several different maneuvers. Within the total concept of multiple defense we have specific maneuvers to combat:

1. The off-tackle play
2. An outside running offense
3. An inside running offense
4. Any other types of plays the opponent has in his offense

This is also true against the passing game. Specific games or maneuvers are included in multiple defense to delay receivers, put pressure on the passer, and provide good coverage.

In this theory of defense we line up in one alignment and on the snap of the ball move and end up in another. We also can jump from one alignment to another alignment on an oral command of the signal caller. We have then two methods of getting to a new defensive alignment. By doing this we are camouflaging our defenses and forcing the offense to find us. They cannot block our linemen until they find them. This confuses the offensive blockers but does not weaken the defense.

Movement on the snap of the ball provides the defense with a weapon to dislodge the advantage the offense has of knowing the starting count.

Using multiple defense allows us to show an apparent weakness—then, on movement, to take it away. Also, the defensive man is not forced to repeat the same maneuver down after down after down. The assurance of having several different games to use is good for the morale of the defensive performer. These factors help build a belief in the defense and establish a strong spirit.

3. *Pass defense men have three types of coverage.*

Pass defense coverages and adjustments will be covered in later chapters. An important fact should be stressed here concerning multiple defenses and the types of coverages that are used: No opposing team can align itself in an offensive formation against us and expect to get the same defensive adjustment each time it uses it. Multiple defense provides flexibility in pass defense coverage and also in making adjustments to various formations. No team can "set" us in the same defense repeatedly. This prevents any team from attempting to or succeeding in taking an individual or the defense "apart." By utilizing the complete repertoire of multiple defense we make this impossible.

4. We play percentages.

An opponent may "hurt" us with a particular play or pass when we are in a certain defensive alignment—but they will not do it repeatedly. When the successful play or pass is repeated we could be in:

    a. another alignment
    b. a different game
    c. another type of pass defense coverage

It is true the offense could make four, eight, or 12 yards against the defense—but next time they could be thrown for a loss. This is also true concerning a pass that was completed. They may attempt to throw the same pass, but by now the entire defense may be changed and we may tackle the passer for a loss, or delay the receiver, or best of all—make an interception. This is what we call *playing percentages.*

The defenses are designed to "bend and not break." They will give on a particular play—but snap back and retaliate on the next play or ensuing series of plays. Multiple defense has been singularly effective in preventing the long run from scrimmage. "Going to the point of responsibility," "reacting to the ball," good release and "proper pursuit" all have aided in preventing the long touchdown jaunt. To keep the long runs to a minimum ALL alignments, games, and coverages must be utilized.

It is very important to keep mixing the defensive calls. In multiple defense it is disastrous to get into a rut and continually call the same defense down after down. No segment of multiple defense is an all-purpose defense. It takes the complete repertoire to accomplish this.

Good Signal Caller Is Requisite for Success of Multiple Defense

Multiple defense is only as strong as the defensive signal caller. Since installing these defenses we have been fortunate in having two particularly adept signal callers: Ronald Champion, All-East center at Penn in 1959, and Alex Kroll, All-American center at Rutgers in 1961. Both these men possessed all the qualities of a good signal caller.

Multiple defense requires a good signal caller because he calls the defenses himself. He is not a messenger boy—but is charged with definite responsibility. Through proper teaching on the field and through indoctrination in defensive quarterback meetings he can be taught to do a good signal calling job. To do this the signal caller must have complete knowledge and understanding of the theory behind multiple defense. He must know the strengths and weaknesses of each defensive alignment, game, and pass defense coverage. Only by possessing this knowledge can he make the correct calls.

The defensive signal caller must have "football sense" and game experience. His decisions cannot be theoretical. He must be battle-tested before assuming the signal calling job.

The boy charged with calling defensive signals must assume the responsibility of studying future opponents. He can do this on his own through movies, scout reports, newspapers, television, and radio. He also will learn about the opponent through player-coach conferences. In addition to knowing the opponent thoroughly he must have a complete knowledge of his own personnel. He cannot become an effective signal caller until he knows his own men.

He must be a forceful leader who exudes true confidence—not the false variety. His teammates must have complete faith in him and respond to his defensive calls. This faith and respect must be earned on the field of battle. No coach can order a team to obey the signal caller. This is something he himself must earn.

When the defensive signal caller makes his call in the huddle his teammates may not doubt him: their job is to execute. When the signal caller says "jump"—they do not ask "why" but "how high"! Only by having complete faith in the defense and the man calling them can multiple defense be successful.

Poise is a basic characteristic that every good signal caller possesses. He must be able to think and react under pressure. Nothing can bother him on the field. He must be in complete charge of the situation.

A good signal caller must "get in rhythm" with the offensive signal caller. Getting rhythm means he is able to anticipate and diagnose what the offensive signal caller is calling—then deploy his own men to meet the threat.

He must continually mix his defensive calls so the offense is forced into errors. He does this by having his men in the right place at the right time. Keep showing the offensive quarterback a different defensive picture each time the ball is snapped. Clever manipulation of defense can break down and destroy the offense.

No Offensive Formation Should Bother
Multiple Defense

The players involved in defense must believe that multiple defense will stop any offense. They must have this belief deeply ingrained in their thinking. A team using multiple defense will never be caught short with only one or two defenses in a game.

Multiple defense provides several different adjustments against the offense's basic formation. In this situation the defense has the advantage and should exploit it. The defense must be taught the strength and weaknesses of the offensive formation.

Good multiple defense can neutralize any strong points the offense possesses. To illustrate this I cite the specific situation of playing against the Belly series. In multiple defense we feel it takes three men to effectively stop the Belly series. We assign a defensive man to the fullback, another to the quarterback, and the third individual to the pitch man (halfback). These responsibilities will change with the different alignments used. Nevertheless, the responsibilities are definite and clear-cut. Because of this our defensive men have a sense of security because they know exactly who is *responsible*.

Teaching Job Is Simplified
by Using Multiple Defense

Multiple defense provides simplified teaching because all alignments, games, pass coverages, and adjustments are taught in pre-season practice. These basic principles of the defense will stay the same throughout the season except for possible minor variations.

There are strong and weak points in each defense. The squad is taught these points when the defense is installed. In doing this, the team acquires greater understanding about the defense. It has been our experience that by doing this the players will react to a known weakness quicker than they normally would. Consequently, the defense is stronger than it theoretically should be.

From each of the three fundamental alignments we teach five or six games. The games have specific names such as: Normal, Pinch, Gap, Red Dog, Basic, Blitz, Eagle, Out, and Over. When we teach a specific game, such as "Pinch," every end, tackle, guard, and linebacker involved is taught exactly what he does in the "Pinch" maneuver. This is done with each of our 15 or 16 games. Every maneuver the boy learns is identified with a specific game and alignment. Ever after the defensive man will know what a "Pinch" game is in contrast to a "Basic" or a "Red Dog" maneuver.

There is no duplication of terms. Specific games are associated with specific alignments. For instance, a "Blitz" is used only from a 53 alignment, while a "Red Dog" game is executed only from a 54 alignment. Using this procedure eliminates the possibility of getting the wrong game called from a specific alignment.

This teaching method facilitates learning. Simplicity is very important. Using this method of teaching we can correct or add defenses without confusion. When a defense is added, a boy can be told: "you do a Pinch," or a "Basic," or an "Out," and he will know exactly what to do because of his previous learning.

We believe that by using a simple numbering system, descriptive nomenclature, and employing the method of teaching that we do, multiple defense can be taught quickly and effectively.

It is readily discernible that we teach individual parts, then assemble the whole or entire defense later. The ends, linemen, and backs are taught, by their respective coaches, what their responsibilities are in a specific defense. This is accomplished during the group work period of practice. Later, in team work, the parts are assembled and the "whole" defense is put together. We go from part to whole in learning to assemble our defenses.

Once the defenses are put together they are drilled and practiced the same as the offense. Our "set-hike" drill has facilitated the learning of multiple defense. Following is an explanation of the drill.

First, we line up our defensive team in that particular alignment (53, 54, 61) which we want to drill against the opponent's offensive formation. The offense is completely immobile, but ready to absorb a blow. The defensive coach calls out the specific game the team is to execute. On the vocal command, "set," they assume their proper stance, then on, "hike," they go to their point of responsibility, deliver the blow, and hold their point. This is done until all games from each alignment are gone through. Corrections can be easily made and mistakes quickly seen. This drill is done for five minutes before the demonstrating team begins to run the opponent's plays into the defense.

Defensive planning, in multiple defense, is one of emphasis. When we are preparing for an opponent the staff goes through our defenses and decides which to use, not to use, or emphasize. Seldom is it necessary to completely discard a defense or to devise a new one. Against a particular opponent, we will emphasize a certain defense, but at no time do we use the same defense continually. This is contrary to the theory of multiple defense and can be damaging to the over-all defense and particularly to the morale of the defensive personnel. One of the strong points of multiple defense is that it is not necessary to devise and learn complete new defenses each week when preparing for a new opponent. This alone warrants consideration for acceptance of multiple defense.

Players Must Have Defensive Pride

Playing defense requires a certain type of boy. He must have a "love for fray," he must like to hit and to get hit. There is a "certain something" about playing defense that brings out real tenacity in a football player.

The defensive unit takes punishment and also gives it. The important factor the defense must learn is that football is a constant struggle—defense versus the offense.

Objective number one, when playing defense, is to defeat the opponent. To do this the offense must be stopped with a minimum gain and be forced into making mistakes. A stout defense can cause the offense to fumble, miss blocking assignments, throw bad passes, and, most important, cause them to lose their poise. A crisp, hard-hitting defensive unit will make reluctant ball carriers out of the offensive backs.

Strong defense wins football games. Also, a game will always remain respectable if the defense is good. A well-worn football cliche says that a good offense is a good defense. The same thing can be said for the reverse of this: *A good defense is a good offense.* There are five ways to score on defense and only three on offense. A good football team should think in terms of scoring when on defense.

Defense is no longer drudgery. In the past a defensive player labored in oblivion but in modern football the defense receives as much public recognition and plaudits as the offense. It takes speed, tenacity, and agility to play defense. These are qualities that appeal to the public and are eye-catching. Ear-catching phrases, radio, and television announcers, and just plain outstanding football players have made the public more conscious of the defensive football player.

A team with strong defense will win the close games. It is important, therefore, to use the theory of multiple defense to develop a spirited, hard-hitting, cohesive, defensive unit.

The Theory

of *Pass Defense*

Chapter Two

EVERY year, since the introduction of the forward pass in football, pass defense has occupied an increasingly important part of the over-all defensive planning of every football team.

Pass defense and all it involves is an exacting and time-consuming task. There are many factors involved in developing and perfecting a sound defense against passes. First, it is important to have boys who possess the fundamental skills necessary to playing good pass defense. In addition, the boys must have, or the coach must instill, a burning desire to excel at this phase of football. When these two qualities are found in a boy, it then takes continuous systematic practice to build a strong pass defense unit. Later in the book a chapter is devoted to the organization and utilization of practice time spent on pass defense.

It is my personal belief that good reactions are more important than unbridled speed in the development of a good pass defender. Speed is important, when playing defense, but it is not the most important quality a boy should possess in order to excel at pass defense. I have found that a boy who has tremendous speed will rely on that speed to get himself out of a jam—after he has been derelict in his duties and made a mistake that got him into trouble. A boy of this type must have his speed disciplined and his ability harnessed so that he can best use his God-given talents for pass defense.

The pass defender who has developed good footwork, which includes the ability to maintain body balance, agility in movement and good reactions—plus mental discipline—develops into a much better defender against passes than the boy who depends on speed alone.

Experience makes a good pass defender outstanding. Assuming that he possesses the qualities mentioned, then experience will make the difference between a good pass defense man and a *great* one.

Basic Concept of Pass Defense

My basic concept of pass defense is *to put pressure on the good passer but not on the poor passer.* We want the inferior passer to throw the ball and put it in the air. He will, without pressure from linemen, over-throw and under-throw his intended receivers a certain percentage of the time— and that percentage works for us.

We want to provide him with the opportunity to pass—so that we can intercept and get possession of the ball. Also, by allowing him to pass, our linemen are free to act as interference when our secondary gets the ball.

Against the fine passer, great pressure must be generated and maintained. Coverage alone will not hold up against the top passer. (Later, in this chapter, I will develop this thought further.) There are three types of coverages used in pass defense. But regardless of which type is used, whether zone, man-for-man or a combination of these two, there is one paramount truth—there is no defense for the *perfect* pass. When the pass is thrown accurately and the receiver makes a good catch, the pass will be completed.

The Theory of Pass Defense

To the pass defense coach or to the boy who takes pride in playing it this statement would be morale-shattering were it not for the fact that specific measures can be taken to hold the number of pass completions to a minimum and prevent a team from "breaking open" a football game.

There are five methods in an over-all pass defense plan which will successfully check and contain the opponent's passing game. No one of the methods can do the job alone, although outstanding success is sometimes realized with a specific maneuver against a particular opponent. Such a situation would be the continual "red-dogging" of a quarterback who, when rushed, is totally ineffective. This fact will emerge when scouting a team or studying their movies.

It is always sound football to use scouting reports to ascertain tendencies of individuals and teams. From these tendencies the type of defensive maneuver to counteract what the opponent likes and can do best may be planned and utilized.

The five factors that can give the defenders the edge in the continual battle between the pass offense and the pass defense are:

1. *Put* pressure on the passer.
2. *Delay* the potential receivers.
3. *Develop* good coverage.
4. *Vary* the defenses, utilize a combination of the first three methods.
5. *Play* for and make pass interceptions.

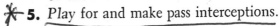 Pressure on the Passer

I am dedicated to the belief that pressure on the passer is the best pass defense. There is nothing that disrupts and destroys a pass offense quicker and more effectively than strong pressure on the passer. There must be seven or even eight men involved if the pressure is to be effective. If fewer men are involved, the offense can block the rushing linemen, then there is neither pressure nor coverage.

Most teams possess a boy who can pass reasonably well when allowed to sit in a rocking chair and throw with no pressure put on him. But it is a different situation when hundreds of pounds of rampaging baby-beef bear down on the passer with the avowed purpose of putting him on his back. It is impossible for a boy to throw from a prone position looking skyward, so an integral part of our pass defense plan is to force the passer to throw from the cellar window, so to speak.

It is important to find out whether the "patter of little feet" bothers the passer to the point of making him so nervous he cannot throw accurately. His reaction to pressure will determine our selection of defenses for the balance of the game or for as long as that particular quarterback is in the game.

When the rush is on, it is necessary to continually drill into your players that the passer must be tackled for a loss or forced to throw the ball hurriedly. This will force him into mistakes, such as throwing off balance, and as a result he will deliver an inaccurate pass. Make the passer do something he does not want or like to do, and cannot do well.

We want the passer gang-rushed and gang-tackled. As the would-be tacklers zero in on the passer they must get their hands in the air, but never leave their feet unless the passer has thrown the ball—and then only in an attempt to block the pass.

Force the passer to throw over the outstretched arms of the rushing tacklers. During the hard-rush maneuver, the linemen must always remain under control so the passer cannot fake a pass, then step around the leaping linemen and deliver the ball. The linemen must make sure when tackling; certainty is more important than how hard the passer is hit.

There is a point to stress concerning rushing linemen: If the passer is facing away from the side of the charging linemen there is no need to raise the hands in the air with the resultant loss of speed. In this situation the linemen must be taught to keep pouring on the steam, continue to rush and penetrate, then bury the shoulder in the passer and put an enthusiastic tackle on him.

When the passer is facing the rushing linemen and plugging linebackers they should tackle the passer *high*, from the top down, so that he cannot get rid of the ball. The men involved in the rush must be aggressive and tenacious—but always under control. In meeting blockers, they must be taught to use head, body and feet fakes in the running battle to get to their quarry. They make contact with the offensive blocker, using the same shoulder and same leg, then get rid of the blocker by controlling his head.

Ends (men with outside defensive responsibilities) must approach from the outside in and always keep leverage. Woe be to your team if the opponent's passer can fake a pass, tuck the ball under his arm and take off for daylight to the outside.

Tackles and guards must be conscious of the draw play, screen pass, Statue of Liberty play and the fake-pass run. An experienced line will handle these changing situations with their quick reactions and football "sense." If experienced linemen are lacking, then good drills simulating game problems will help inexperienced boys gain the necessary poise to handle the situation.

A well-trained, disciplined line that charges hard is the best pass defense. At Rutgers, under the tutelage of line coach Warren Schmakel, we have had good line play. This was true also at the University of Pennsylvania, in 1959, where C. A. "Tim" Temerario was in charge of the defense and Bernie Lemonick coached the interior defensive line. That year Penn ranked seventh nationally in rushing defense and was outstanding in pass defense. Success in rushing defense usually means success in pass defense and vice versa; they complement each other.

When pressure is put on the passer, one or more of the linebackers must be involved. But they cannot put heat on the passer and *also* provide coverage; they must have one or the other. Others must assume their coverage responsibilities when they are part of the rush.

Coaches must make players understand that when extreme pressure is being put on, with seven or eight men, coverage is sacrificed for the hard rush. With linebackers rushing, a secondary receiver may be open temporarily, but an end is assigned to cover him in this situation. Also, with eight men putting pressure on the passer we expect them to tackle the passer before he throws the ball or at least force an inaccurate pass.

In summation: when putting pressure on the passer, we have four objectives, they are:

1. *Hurry* the passer, force him into mistakes.

2. *Block* the pass.
3. *Tackle* the passer, with the ball, for a loss.
4. *Get* the interception.

Delay the Potential Receivers

The rules allow the defense to block, jam or shove the potential receiver until the ball is thrown. The opposite defensive men involved in these maneuvers must jam the offensive end and force him to the outside. This prevents him from getting downfield quickly against the deep secondary defender. It also helps reduce chances for the quick or diagonal pass.

It is easier and more effective to hold up ends from either an inside or outside position rather than head-on. Delaying the ends in this manner cuts to a minimum the opportunity they have to fake the defensive man. Lining up on the inside means the linebacker takes a position on the inside shoulder of the offensive end. An outside position means the linebacker assumes a defensive stance on the outside shoulder of the offensive end.

All offensive personnel are potential blockers, until the ball is thrown, and defensive men are thus permitted to use their hands against them. The man on defense cannot hold—but a good jolt will disturb the balance of the potential receiver and will help upset the pattern he wants to run. It will also ruin the timing of the play by costing him at least one step. Regardless whether the potential receiver is on the line of scrimmage or downfield, we want him played aggressively until the ball is thrown; then our men fly to the ball with equal tenacity and aggressiveness.

A word of caution regarding delaying receivers. It is difficult for one man to delay an end for any length of time. It is impossible, in fact, if the end is put out wide as a spread end. This should be considered when making defensive plans to delay receivers. The maneuvers necessary for delaying receivers, other than spread ends, include line loops, slants, pinching ends and eagle-type linebackers. Eagle linebackers, of course, are those that line up either head-on the end or on either shoulder and give the end a jolt as he attempts to go out for a pass. If your available personnel cannot execute any of these specific maneuvers properly, then it is best to discard that particular movement and concentrate on other methods of delaying the potential receivers. This will continue, of course, until the men involved in these maneuvers can be taught to execute properly. The linemen and linebacker need not be perfect at a specific technique, such as slants or jamming ends, before using it.

It is questionable whether linemen are more effective at delaying the receiver or concentrating 100 percent on getting to the passer with reckless abandon. They cannot do both simultaneously— either one or the other must be stressed in a specific maneuver or defensive game. It is difficult to delay clever receivers without holding them. It requires an excellent defensive man to play against a clever offensive performer and achieve the desired results. The decision regarding what to do must be dictated by the personnel available.

Eagle-type linebackers can get so involved in delaying a receiver they forget their pass coverage responsibilities. This will allow a back, on a pass pattern away from the strength or flow, to run loose. *This we do not want.*

All these factors must enter into the decision of whether or not to delay the receivers and how much.

Develop Good Coverage

Regardless of the type of coverage used, in order to contain good receivers and a good passer, both pressure on the passer and good coverage must be used. It is unwise to rely solely on coverage when playing against a good passer. He must have pressure too. There are three fundamental types of coverage in pass defense:

1. Zone
2. Man-for-man
3. Combination of man-for-man and zone

I will briefly cover the theory of each coverage and also their strengths and weaknesses.

Zone. The strength of zone coverage is against deep passes; very few long passes are completed against it. Also, a slower boy is more effective in the zone than in man-for-man pass defense.

In zone coverage each defensive man has a particular zone to cover against passes. The defensive men key the uncovered offensive linemen. Once the ball is snapped they will show by their blocking immediately whether or not it is to be a pass. On a running play the linemen fire out and block aggressively; on passes, they drop back to protect. When it is a pass the defensive backs will drop into the middle of their respective zones, all the while watching the passer. The receivers coming downfield are not as important to the defender as the passer with the ball. In straight zone coverage, the defensive man never leaves his zone to cover a man. He only leaves it to go for the ball. When the ball is thrown he gives it his undivided attention. He becomes a centerfielder. Very good reaction to the ball is of the utmost importance in developing a strong zone pass defense. Zone coverage succeeds or fails on the ability of the pass defenders *to anticipate the pass.* They cannot wait until the ball leaves the passer's hands to react; they must be on their way by then. Consequently, zone defenders are taught to watch the passer's eyes. Where he looks he will throw. Very few passers can look in one direction and throw accurately in another.

Against flanked backs or spread ends the straight zone coverage can still be used. When defending their own goal line most zone pass defenses convert to man-for-man coverage.

The weakness of the zone pass defense is that it can be exploited by putting three or four receivers into the same zone; if no help arrives, then one defender must cover all four men. Also, in zone coverage it is difficult to cover the flat, short and hook passes. When deep men drop back immediately to cover passes, and the linemen are rushing the passer, the middle area is exposed to hook, crossing and square-out pass patterns.

Another zone weakness appears when the passer has plenty of time to throw. The zones then become too large for one man to cover; in fact when the offensive pass protection holds up there is actually no such thing as a zone defense. The longer the passer is able to hold the ball the further away and apart the receivers spread as they run their patterns. Now the zone defenders are forced into man-for-man coverage because they react only to the ball and it is still in the passer's hands. When potential

The Theory of Pass Defense

receivers run through the zones, the defenders must pick them up and cover them. The defenders are forced, under these circumstances, to forget their zones and cover the man. Also, when no receiver comes into a defender's zone—he is wasted because the zone defender reacts only to the ball.

In zone coverage the men involved do not have specific responsibilities; therefore they should not and cannot react to fakes too quickly.

When throwing against the zone, the passer must be aware that he is attempting to beat the defense and not the individual.

Man-for-man. Each player involved in man-for-man coverage is assigned to a specific potential receiver. He covers that individual wherever he goes. Assignments are clear-cut and specific. There must never be any doubt regarding responsibilities or coverage. No defensive man should ever be fooled as to the identity of his man. In this type of coverage no one is wasted in an area where there are no potential receivers. When playing man-for-man it is possible to get more men rushing the passer. Under most circumstances it provides a greater number of defenders to play the ball. Another strong point: it is possible to put the best pass defender against the opponent's top receiver.

But there are certain inherent weaknesses in man-for-man coverage. First, there are only a limited number of defensive performers who possess the ability to cover one man all over the field. A good receiver can be pitted against an inept defender. Even more of a problem: a clever receiver has the opportunity to outmaneuver an individual pass defender despite the fact that he might be outstanding on defense. In man-for-man coverage, it is imperative to be constantly aware of the crossing patterns and decoy routes that the receivers will attempt to establish.

In all pass defense, and particularly in man-for-man coverage, the defensive man must play the pass *first* and the run *second*. If the actions of the pass receiver, even on the running play, indicate a potential pass, the pass defender must respect this maneuver and stay back. As a result he cannot react fast enough to be of help against the run.

When the opposing end blocks, the defender cannot "fire up" to the line of scrimmage to make the tackle. If he does, he will be beaten deep on the next play by an alert offense when the end blocks for three counts then releases for the deep pass. This will occur when the defender reacts to the block too quickly and comes up to make the tackle. On pass defense, it is much better to stand still than to commit too fast.

Anyone playing man-for-man should, and must, know that the passer is attempting to beat an isolated man and not the entire coverage. Due to the nature of the coverage, the offense will attempt to isolate one man and beat him rather than attack the entire man-for-man coverage with specific patterns.

Combination man-for-man coverage. There are several types of combination pass defense coverage. Certain combination defenses will have specific defenders cover man-for-man while simultaneously the other defensive man will play a zone. Another type is to have man-for-man responsibilities within the framework of a zone. Still another combination coverage is to start with a zone and have man-for-man responsibilities within the confines of the zone.

The Theory of Pass Defense

Needless to say, this type of coverage gives the pass defenders various and alternating responsibilities. Combination coverage requires poise, cleverness and ability to adjust rapidly to a given situation. The defenders must be able to react quickly to avoid confusion and must possess the thorough knowledge of their assignments and responsibilities which comes with experience. When the pass defenders are sure of their specific duties and principles, the combination man-for-man and zone coverage is the soundest and the most effective type of pass defense.

Vary the Defenses, Use Combination of First Three Methods

It was stated in Chapter One that we use multiple defense, with games and play percentages. This is also true of pass defense. Within the framework of our defenses there are games devised to:

✓**a.** put pressure on the passer
✓**b.** delay the receiver
✓ **c.** get single and double coverage

This is done to accomplish what we want in a specific situation. We do not rely 100 percent on any one of those three maneuvers but will always keep mixing our defensive calls so that our pass defense coverage will not be readily discernible to the opponent. The opponent must not know what to expect; he must be kept guessing.

Against these continually changing defensive calls, the opponent must forecast the type of coverage being used on a coming play, probe that coverage to find the weakness, then catch us in the particular one they hope to defeat. When this is accomplished the opponent then must determine how to attack the coverage with the passes they have at their disposal; next they must get the correct passes called and executed properly—all at precisely the right time!

The percentages are in our favor and we believe in exploiting this fact.

Play for and Get Interceptions

We put great emphasis on getting interceptions. We are not content just to knock the ball down. Interceptions are stressed to the extent that we want our pass defenders to usually intercept on fourth down and *always* on third down. We do not want the ball knocked to the ground on third down only to see, on the next play, a long pass completed for a touchdown. This has happened!

Many passes are completed, for touchdowns and long yardage, on an "obvious punt situation." Consequently, we go for the third down interception and take that punt situation away. We want the ball—always and anywhere. Until the pass defenders acquire the habit of intercepting, we teach our men to intercept every pass they can possibly get near, regardless of the tactical situation or field position. When going for the interception we cannot have any mental stuttering. *Get the football!*

Once a pass defender acquires experience and good football sense then we allow him to use his judgment about intercepting on fourth down situations. The deployment of his own teammates at the time of the interception, position and condition of field are other factors that enter into his decision whether to intercept or knock the ball down.

Interceptions can and do win football games.

The Theory of Pass Defense

They do more to break a team's morale than any one factor in football. In 1961 Rutgers defeated Colgate 26-6. Three of the four touchdowns that we scored were made or set up by pass interceptions. Safetyman Sam Mudie returned two for touchdowns of 52 and 38 yards respectively. His third interception was returned 27 yards to the Colgate two yard line. Two plays later Rutgers scored. With the 117 yards gained on his three interceptions, Mudie had the leading single game performance of any defensive back in the nation for the 1961 season. Pass interceptions *do* win football games.

They also can be and often are turning points in football games.

Interceptions can equal 14 points. Take a situation where an intended receiver is in the open and ready to catch a sure-fire touchdown pass but at the last instant a defensive back intercepts the ball and returns it for a touchdown—this is an interception that is worth 14 and possibly 16 points. Interceptions are equal to blocked punts and also remove punts. Tactically speaking, a blocked punt is worth 40 yards and possession of the ball. An interception can result in the same advantage to the defensive team.

Once the ball is in the air—it is ours. After it has been thrown, we tell our pass defenders to "fly to the ball"—it is the only one in the game and once it is thrown, it will not change direction.

When making the interception we stress going for the ball with both hands and arms fully extended. We tell defenders, "Never put the hands on the opponent's body." Using this technique makes it impossible to be called for pass interference.

During the actual act of intercepting the pass, we emphasize the following points:

1. Go through the man to get the ball.
2. Look the ball into your hands.
3. Catch the ball at its highest point.
4. After the ball is caught, call out the oral signal, and put it away.
5. Dig hard for three steps and head for the goal line. (Note the photographic sequence in *Figure 4*.)

When the passer throws the ball and the interception is made, every team member, except the man blocking the potential receiver, sets up a running course so he will be in position to form interference for the interceptor. An example of this happened in the Rutgers-Bucknell game of 1961. Safetyman Bill Speranza returned an interception 55 yards for a touchdown. When he crossed the Bucknell 10-yard line he was escorted by six of his Rutgers teammates.

Considerable time is devoted to blocking for the interceptor following an interception. Drills are devised to simulate game conditions so that all team members will react immediately, in a *positive* manner, to an interception. Particularly do we emphasize that the man nearest to the interceptor block and knock down the intended receiver. This is done for a reason. I conducted a survey and found that on 90 percent of the interceptions the man making the interception was tackled by the potential receiver, thus destroying any opportunity for a long return. We seek to eliminate that potential receiver—once the interception is made. In Chapter Nine, devoted to drills, this maneuver will be discussed in detail.

Figure 4: Yaksick vs. Columbia

We do everything possible, on every forward pass that is thrown, to encourage the eleven defensive men to be alert to the possibility of a pass interception. In the event they are unable to tackle the passer, it is imperative that all rushing linemen turn and follow the flight of the ball. They must be ready to block when the interception is made.

When the ball is thrown to the left our linemen move to that side; when it is thrown to the right they move in that direction, and when it is thrown down the middle they turn and start throwing blocks. The boy making the interception will make the decision where to run. Basically, we try to establish a threat to the inside, then go for the sidelines. There is a defensive weakness in this area. Touchdowns scored here are easy scores because the defenses are loosely organized. Naturally, if an interceptor sees daylight, he will disregard his rules and run for the obvious open area.

I believe in using the pass interception as an offensive weapon.

Psychological

Factors in *Pass Defense*

Chapter Three

PLAYING pass defense is very important and a singular honor. The boy who has the opportunity to play pass defense must know it is a privilege to be a part of the defensive unit. It is a challenge to play defense and it is fun.

My Philosophy of Pass Defense

I seek to instill these facts into the boy who desires to be a pass defender. It is a challenge because backs are chosen first for their offensive ability —they must *learn* defense. Some boys have a particular ability for defense. Their ability must be harnessed and disciplined. Others are not adept at defense. The challenge here is to develop these boys into strong pass defenders by hard work. If they have a burning desire to excel at pass defense, it can be done.

Defensive players must have a deep-seated drive from within to be outstanding pass defenders. They must take the job seriously and do everything possible to improve themselves in mastery of fundamentals and precise execution.

It is mandatory that each individual involved in pass defense seek to improve himself. He can do this by working on fundamentals, agility, reaction, self-discipline, and body position on the potential receiver.

In my personal opinion, the true measure of good pass defense is the number of interceptions, yards gained on interception, returns, and touchdowns scored compared to the yards gained and touchdowns scored by the opponent on pass offense.

Build a Belief

We use the positive approach in our pass defense. We build a belief among the boys concerning the type of pass defense coverage we use. There are no negative thoughts about "holding them" on pass defense. We want an aggressive, positive attitude and we sell the boys on this very strongly.

No one is going to win games by throwing on us. If they do connect for one, then we hope that they will throw again—so we can get the ball.

Our pass defense men are told quite accurately that they will not face many top-flight passers in college football. When we do face a really good passer, he will pass the ball perfectly only six or seven times in a game. He may "hit" a certain percentage—but when one bad pass comes we are going to intercept and get the ball. We expect to intercept as least one of every eight passes thrown at us.

Maintaining poise is all-important when playing pass defense. We teach our men that nothing can happen on the football field which we cannot handle. Individual pass defenders or the entire pass defense never can lose confidence and poise, regardless of what happens. When the pass defenders begin to worry about or doubt any one segment of pass defense—the next step is to become tense and "freeze." When this happens the pass defense men will not be able to react properly to the ball and as a result the pass defense will disintegrate.

Building a belief concerning pass defense is important. Dare the opponent to throw—so the defense can get the ball.

To aid us in building a belief in the pass de-

Psychological Factors in Pass Defense

fense and also to challenge the pass defenders we have an *Interception Chart*. The chart, shown in *Figure 5*, is placed on the wall of the dressing room at the beginning of each football season. The following items are listed on the chart:

1. Our interception goal for the season.

Check This out

2. Our player making the interception; the opponent—his number of pass completions, attempts, yards gained, touchdowns scored on passes.

3. We tabulate our interceptions, yards they were returned, and touchdowns scored against the opponent's attempts, completions, yardage, and touchdowns. We compare the opponent's passing yardage against our interception yardage.

4. Cumulative statistics are kept on all facts that appear on the chart. A quick look at the chart can tell us:

a. Our total number of interceptions, yards returned, and touchdowns.

b. Our interceptions, yards returned, and touchdowns scored versus each specific opponent.

c. Which players have made the interceptions.

d. How many each player has made.

e. Each opponent's pass attempts, completions, yards gained, and touchdowns.

f. Our opponent's totals in all the aforementioned categories.

g. Opponent's total attempts and our total interceptions.

PASS INTERCEPTIONS

TEAM INTER-CEPTIONS	PLAYER	INDIVIDUAL INTERCEPTION	OPPONENT	OUR: COMP. ATTS. YDG. TD's	OUR: YDG. INTER. RETURNED TD's	-WE- INTER. YDG. RETURNED TD's (CUMULATIVE)	-THEY- ATTEMPTS YDG. GAINED TD's (CUMULATIVE)
1	MUDIE	1	SIWASH TECH	3 11 27 0	3 28 1	3 28 1	11 27 0
2	DOELLING	1					
3	BOLDEN	1					
						INTERCEPTIONS: 3 OF 11 = 1 OF 3.7	
4	YAKSICK	1	NORTH DAKOTA	4 16 48 1	3 21 0	6 49 1	27 75 1
5	HANLON	1					
6	TERPAK	1					
						INTERCEPTIONS: 6 OF 27 = 1 OF 4.5	
7	LOWE	1	PAINTED POST	0 9 0 0	3 29 1	9 78 2	36 75 1
8	YAKSICK	2					
9	BOLDEN	2					
						INTERCEPTIONS: 9 OF 36 = 1 OF 4	
10	DOELLING	2	SILVER SPRINGS	7 21 81 1	4 47 1	12 125 3	57 156 2
11	BYRD	1					
12	RIEPL	1					
						INTERCEPTIONS: 12 OF 57 = 1 OF 4.7	
13	RIEPL	2	ST. ANDREWS	2 12 14 0	2 4 0	14 129 3	69 170 2
14	FRAUENHEIM	1					
						INTERCEPTIONS: 14 OF 69 = 1 OF 4.9	
15	KOWALSKI	1	PACIFIC U.	14 34 181 2	1 32 1	15 161 4	103 351 4
						INTERCEPTIONS: 15 OF 103 = 1 OF 6.9	
16	KROLL	1	LUTHER	1 21 8 0	5 164 1	20 325 5	124 359 4
17	CHAMPION	1					
18	MUDIE	2					
19	COFFIN	1					
20	MUDIE	3					
						INTERCEPTIONS: 20 OF 124 = 1 OF 6.2	
21	PARKS	1	SYLVANIA TECH	4 18 80 1	2 11 1	22 336 6	132 439 5
22	KOZE	1					
						INTERCEPTIONS: 22 OF 132 = 1 OF 6	
			TOTAL—	35 132 439 5	22 336 6	INTERCEPTIONS: 22 OF 132 = 1 OF 6	

Figure 5: Interception Chart

A statement of challenge to the pass defense—"We must intercept 1 of every 8 passes thrown at us"—is at the bottom of the chart.

We have found that the *Interception Chart*, with the readily available statistics, is very helpful in building a belief regarding our pass defense.

Develop an Esprit de Corps

All great fighting units have a strong *esprit de corps*. Every player must take personal pride in playing and having success on defense. It is a privilege and honor to play pass defense.

We are on defense to get the football. (In 1961 our opponents gained 884 yards in passing—we returned interceptions for 405 yards.) We seek to build a "bond of loyalty" amongst the pass defense men. It takes a good man to play in such exclusive company. Once a player becomes a part of a pass defense unit which possesses this spirit, he too feels and acts this way. Build a strong *esprit de corps*. It leads directly to a feeling of cohesiveness and strength. This is what we want.

We sell our players on the idea that good pass defense is actually an offensive weapon. Playing pass defense with a defensive unit that has a strong *esprit de corps* is a privilege and each boy who becomes a part of this tightly knit group senses this fact. It permeates him. He loses himself in something that is bigger than himself.

There are several factors involved in building a sound pass defense, but none is more important than the psychological factor. The boys must want to play and be ready to play at game time.

We have done two things which have helped significantly in attaining this important psychological factor—which in turn has helped the pass defense to achieve success: (1) We give a star to each player and paste it on his helmet for every pass that he intercepts. (2) We adopted a unique word for an oral signal, discussed later in this chapter, which is shouted out when a player gets a pass interception.

Figure 6 shows student manager Tony Oliva pasting the seventh star for the 1961 season on safetyman Sam Mudie's helmet. The stars are kept on the sidelines during the game. When a player makes an interception the star is pasted on his helmet, by the student manager, the next time he comes out of the game.

Awarding stars for interceptions has been a motivating influence in getting more interceptions and also a strong morale factor. The actual awarding of stars may be original, but the concept was borrowed from the pages of the glorious history that General Claire Chennault and his Flying Tigers wrote during their air battles with the Japanese over Burma and China during the early days of World War II.

When a Flying Tiger shot down an enemy plane, a miniature Japanese plane was painted on the fuselage of his plane. Major Gregory "Pappy" Boyington and his "Black Sheep" squadron followed this practice as did many others later.

It was my thought that if painting a miniature enemy plane on fuselages for each enemy shot out of the skies in wartime was good, then a star pasted on the helmet of each pass defender getting an interception in football during peace time would also be good. It has been.

We believe in psychological warfare.

Figure 6

"Jericho"—Our Oral Signal
for Pass Interceptions

In Chapter Two it was stated that we put great emphasis on getting pass interceptions.

Pass defense can be an offensive weapon when the defense concentrates on getting interceptions. It is my firm conviction that until a team develops an intense desire to intercept the ball and takes pride in how many it intercepts, a team will not get many interceptions. Getting the ball must be paramount in their minds. In everything we do on defense we stress getting interceptions. Once we began to stress interceptions it was necessary to have an oral signal to inform the team an interception had been made and that we were now on offense. This means every team member must immediately begin throwing blocks for the interceptor.

I wanted a word that would be emphatic, easily pronounced, and would have a "ring of positiveness." Most important—a word was desired that would be a "battle cry." After considerable thought a word emerged that possessed all the previously stated qualifications.

That word was JERICHO. It is a Biblical term and that is as it should be because the Bible is read daily in our home. The story of Joshua and the Battle of Jericho closely approximated what was wanted for a word that would be a battle cry. *Hebrews* 11:30 says, "By faith the walls of Jericho fell down . . ." We wanted to instill exactly this positive thinking into the pass defense personnel. They must have faith that they will get interceptions (Jerichoes), must have faith that they will re-

Mustang

Psychological Factors in Pass Defense

turn them for yardage as well as for touchdowns.

The word Jericho was added to our pass defense nomenclature. It immediately caught on. The players took to it, as did the newspaper writers. In a short time the word interception disappeared from the squad's vocabulary and Jericho replaced it. No one on our football team refers to an interception as anything but a Jericho. When our players watch a football game and someone makes an interception—invariably the comment is made "he got a Jericho."

The word has become an important symbol. It points up my precept regarding the importance of intercepting the ball when playing pass defense. In all our pass defense work, be it drills, practice, or in a game, whenever a player gets his hands on the football he calls out "Jericho." This is so deeply imbedded in him, through constant drilling, that shouting the word is a reaction.

We devised and named a drill for the word. The Jericho Drill is one of our best and most used drills. It helped us immeasurably in establishing a nation-leading 1961 total of 405 yards and 4 touchdowns on Jericho returns.

In the drill we stress the importance of knocking down the potential receiver once the ball is Jerichoed. The defender nearest the interceptor throws the key block. The drill is explained in detail in Chapter Nine, which is devoted entirely to pass defense drills.

Eventually the word Jericho permeated the vocabulary of the student body. In the past year applicants for *Scarlet Key*, an honorary service fraternity at Rutgers, were surprised to find that one of the questions they must answer in order to be accepted into this exclusive group was: "What is a Jericho?"

Suffice it to say, the word has been good for us. Call it a gimmick or whatever you wish—it has done and is doing the job we want it to do. That, of course, is to help the pass defense get more Jerichoes!

Ten Basic

Principles of

Our *Pass Defense*

Chapter Four

OUR pass defense is a combination of man-for-man and zone coverage. Everyone in our pass defense has definite responsibilities from the instant the ball is snapped.

What we actually do is use individual man-for-man defensive fundamentals and techniques within a zone. This not only strengthens the zone but also makes it possible to use a man-for-man coverage when it is wanted and needed. It is my humble opinion that man-for-man pass defense coverage is absolutely necessary in the development of good pass defenders. This is true as long as this point is stressed: the defender must cover the offensive man until the ball is in the air—then play the ball 100 percent.

Our thoughts regarding pass defense have developed and evolved over a twenty-year period. Our ideas are not based on theory but practicability. They have been hammered out on the "anvil of experience." It is my belief that experience is the best teacher. *Experience is a hard teacher because it gives the test first, the lesson later.* Something learned from actual experience has a habit of being retained; particularly is this true when that "something" is learned in the heat of battle.

Our pass defense is built on a set of 10 basic principles. Everything we do on pass defense evolves from these principles. Following are the 10 principles that we teach and the order in which they are taught:

1. Know *alignment* and *stance.*
2. *Identify* opponent's *formations.*

3. Know *adjustments* to opponent's formations.
4. Know who the *potential long receivers* are.
5. Know the *keys*.
6. Know what *flow* means.
7. Know what *pre-determine* means.
8. Know what *eye-control* is and what responsibilities are.
9. Know what the *maze* is.
10. Maintain *verbal communication*. Remember the cardinal rule of pass defense: *No one gets behind you.*

In Chapters Five and Six, which are devoted to three-deep (special) and four-deep (box) coverage, I will discuss in detail each of these principles in relation to the specific type of coverage. This chapter will cover the 10 principles in relation to the over-all aspect of our pass defense.

Alignment and Stance

We teach and use both the three-deep and four-deep types of pass defense coverage. This is done because we feel that both are necessary to complete pass defense coverage. Four potential long receivers demand four deep defenders to cover them. There are some pass patterns that three-deep coverage cannot cover adequately, such as a double hook, double swing pattern. Also, there are certain pass patterns that three-deep coverage will cover better and with more definite responsibilities. Both types of coverage are needed.

It is necessary at this time to emphasize a point regarding our pass defense. We deploy our secondary men in *two* fundamental alignments (three- and four-deep), but we use *three* types of coverage. The words secondary alignment and coverage are not synonymous.

In our system of multiple defense, as discussed in Chapter One, it was stated that we use both the 53 and 54 fundamental defensive alignments. The 53 alignment requires a three-deep secondary, while the 54 alignment with two inside linebackers needs a four-deep coverage, although we have used three-deep coverage in a 54 alignment. Using multiple defense makes learning both three- and four-deep coverages mandatory.

Every player involved in pass defense is taught a specific stance which he uses in each of the two pass defense alignments that we teach. Stance will be covered in detail, in Chapters Five and Six, where our two pass defense alignments are discussed. Basically, we teach the parallel stance for inside linebackers and safetymen in both three and four deep, because we want them to move laterally on their first move. It is my conviction that a parallel stance permits the lateral move without taking a false step first.

The defensive halfbacks (three deep) and corner linebackers (four deep) are taught to keep their "outside leg free"—which means the outside leg is back and the inside leg is up toward the line of scrimmage.

We never want a defensive man to have his hands on his knees or to be standing erect when the ball is snapped. Never does he "anchor himself to the ground," by putting weight on his knees, through the simple and sometimes subconscious maneuver of putting his hands on his knees.

Ill Def
favor inside

An important part of pass coverage is *position on the receiver* regardless of the alignment, stance, or coverage used. Our pass defenders are taught never to line up "head-on" with an offensive back or end. Lining up head-on gives the offensive man two directions he can go. The defenders must position themselves so they are on either the inside or outside shoulder of the potential receiver. By positioning themselves either inside or outside, the defenders limit the direction that the intended receiver can go. Field position will dictate whether to be in an inside or an outside position.

We also teach a six-yard sideline rule. No defensive back assumes his stance closer than six yards to the sideline—regardless of where the potential receiver for whom he is responsible stations himself. It is imperative that the defender have good position both before and after the ball is snapped. He must line up correctly, then, when the ball is snapped, keep himself in a position to look through the receiver to the passer. *Keep leverage on the potential receiver.* Leverage means getting and maintaining good vertical and lateral position on the intended receiver. This way he can do a better job of playing the ball and getting the all-important interception. A defender who plays the ball when it is thrown can frequently cover up an error in alignment and stance by either himself or a fellow pass defender.

In addition to the two types of coverage, three-deep (special) and four-deep (box), mentioned previously, we also teach a third type—box-set coverage. By adding the word "set" (which means ignore flow) we have a third type of coverage. This coverage is the true four-deep zone pass defense. It will be explained in Chapter Six.

We teach, practice, and use all three types of pass defense coverage mentioned in this chapter.

Identify the Opponent's Formations

Earlier in the book it was stated that the defensive signal caller calls the defenses, including the pass defense coverage. After he has made his call and the opponent has set himself in a specific formation at the line of scrimmage—our safety man, who is the offensive quarterback, repeats the pass defense coverage (special, box, or box-set), then identifies the opponent's offensive formation and its direction (right or left).

The quarterback and no one else has this responsibility. He is the captain of the pass defense. What he calls is correct. In the system of formation identification that we use, the safetyman identifies the offensive backs first and, if need be, the line second. To avoid confusion—no one else calls out any words. It is extremely important that the safety man identify the offensive formations correctly because our defensive men make specific adjustments, depending on his call, to each offensive formation.

(On pages 88 to 89, Figure 7, are listed different offensive formations and the word that is used to identify each. These formations are taught to all pass defenders, and particularly to the safetyman on the field.)

Know Adjustments to Opponent's Formations

Once the defensive signal caller has called the defense and the safety man has identified the offensive formation, the defensive personnel make their adjustments.

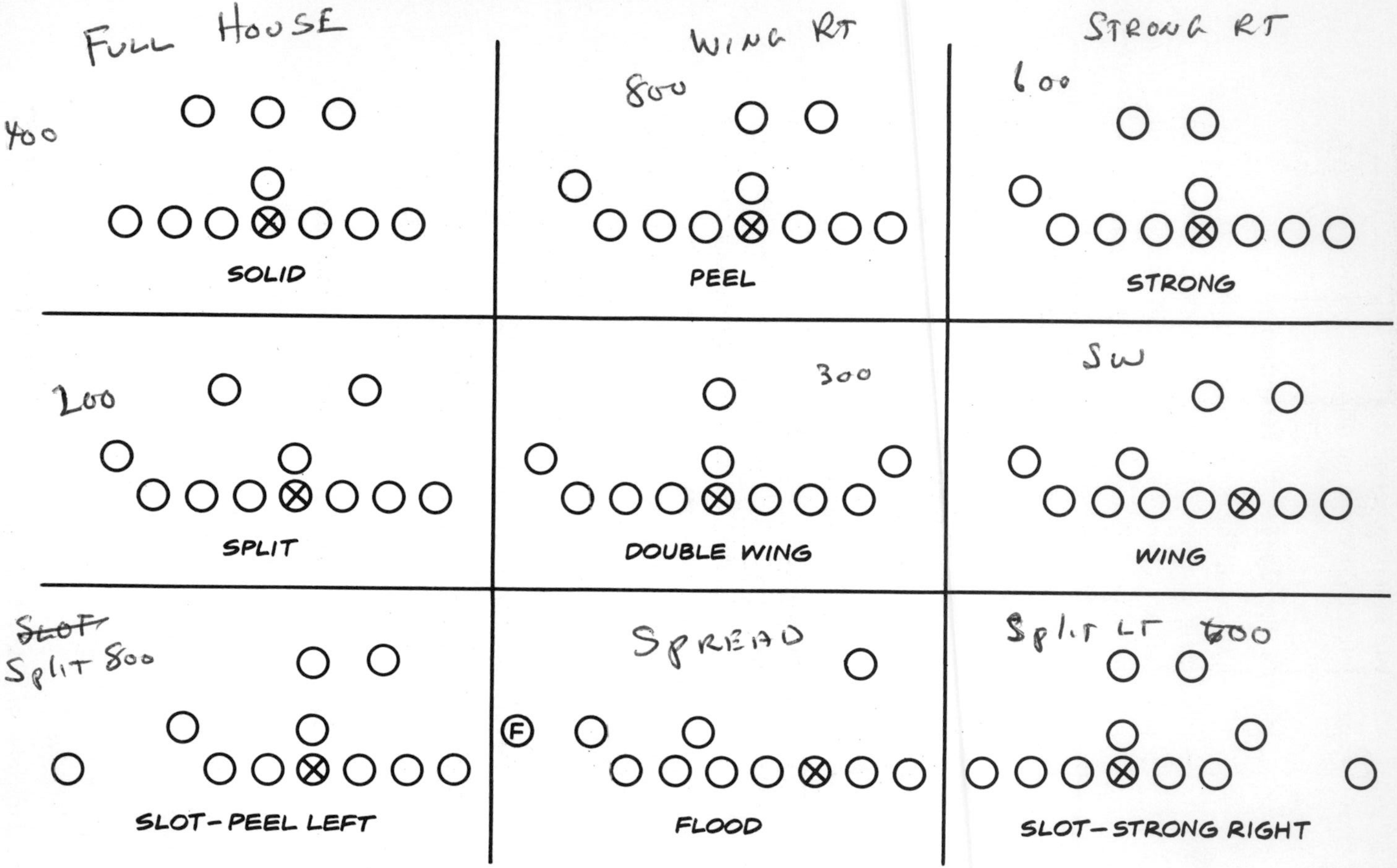
FULL HOUSE
400
SOLID
WING RT
800
PEEL
STRONG RT
600
STRONG
200
SPLIT
300
DOUBLE WING
SW
WING
SLOT
Split 800
SLOT-PEEL LEFT
SPREAD
F
FLOOD
Split LT 600
SLOT-STRONG RIGHT

Figure 7

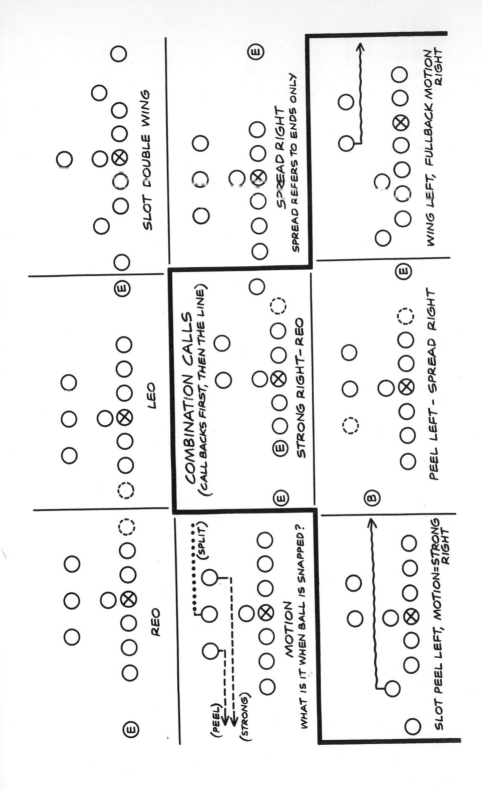

Each man involved in pass defense learns a set of principles from each of the three fundamental defensive alignments that he reacts to when making adjustments against different offensive formations. In addition to the adjustments the defense makes from a particular defense they also learn the ratio that a specific adjustment is to be used. This again is part of our over-all defensive planning, which includes playing percentages, as discussed in Chapter One.

Basically, our adjustments are: backs adjust to backs, linebackers and ends to ends. Our adjustments from both the three- and four-deep secondary alignments will be discussed in later chapters.

Pass defense men, including linebackers, ends, and "invert" men must know the equidistance position and rule. An invert man is an inside safety in a four-deep secondary alignment who positions himself four yards from the line of scrimmage rather than the customary eight. The equidistance position is the spot a defensive man stations himself when an offensive end is spread or a back flanker is four yards or more from the end man on his scrimmage line. The defensive man positions himself laterally halfway between the widest offensive receiver and the receiver's teammate lined up closest to him on the line of scrimmage. After the defender takes this position he backs up to a point three yards or more off the line. This places him vertically at a 45 degree angle to the inside of the widest potential receiver. This is the equidistance position which all pass defense personnel must learn and know.

The single most important rule regarding adjustments is that pass defenders must talk to each other. They must continually reaffirm their responsibilities from their different coverages against the opponent's offensive formations. The defensive personnel will never make a mistake in making adjustments if they talk to each other at all times.

Know the Potential Long Receivers

The deep pass defenders must develop a "sense of security" against long passes. Knowing who the potential long receivers are helps provide the secondary men with this feeling of security. Depending upon the type of coverage be it three or four-deep—the pass defenders must know who the potential three and four long receivers are.

Regardless of the coverage used, the offensive ends are automatically two of the three potential long receivers; the third would be the first back out of the backfield. He could come from a flanker position or from a solid backfield formation. We teach our three-deep secondary men that they are always responsible for the three potential long receivers.

It is necessary that the pass defenders know the difference between the number of potential long receivers when using three-deep coverage in contrast to four-deep.

In four-deep coverage the four potential long receivers—two of which are the offensive ends—belong to the four deep defenders. There can be no doubt or indecision about the defenders' responsibilities in both coverages, regarding the identity of the potential three and four long receivers.

Know the Keys

The offensive backs are our keys. The backs tell us immediately whether it is a solid or flanker formation and what type of flanker formation. The pass defenders must *always* know which alignment and coverage they are in and using—plus the opponent's formation.

This is mandatory because the pass defenders have different and specific keys—from the three types of coverage that we use—against the opponent's solid and flanker formations. Keys are important to some types of pass defenses because they give the pass defender a "jump" in ascertaining whether the play is a pass or run. We react to all plays as passes until the run is definitely established —consequently we are not concerned with this type of keying as much as others. We want to determine immediately the direction the backs are going. For this reason we key backs very hard.

Know What Flow Means

We play flow when the offense is in a solid formation. Flow is determined by the direction in which the offensive backs whom we are keying move. We key for flow against the solid formation from both our three- and four-deep coverage—but our keys are different in each coverage that is used. Determining flow is very important to our type of pass defense because of the flexibility in responsibilities we want in our coverage. We will not be forced into the situation where we have to commit ourselves—before the ball snaps—as to how we are covering the opponent's passes. Therefore we play flow and have specific keys that determine this for us.

Know What Pre-Determine Means

Pre-determine means that the strength of the defensive secondary alignment has been decided either to the right or the left, before the ball is snapped. We can pre-determine strength based on personnel, field position, or formation strength on a call from the pass defense captain. Whichever situation prevails, the strength of the formation has been "pre-determined," and our defensive secondary will make an adjustment accordingly. When we pre-determine against a particular formation we ignore flow. In the past we have pre-determined against a solid formation, using an oral signal, in addition to flankered formation—but in modern football we pre-determine only against specific flanker formations. The decision to pre-determine depends on the type of pass patterns the opponent runs from a particular flanker formation.

Know What Eye-Control Is and What Responsibilities Are

Eye-control is the self-discipline a pass defender must force on himself to focus his eyes on the backs that are being keyed. When the keys move, the defensive man must react to what his eyes tell him and go to his specific responsibilities. Direction is determined when the offensive backs move two steps either right or left. Once direction takes place the defender need no longer focus on the offensive backs.

Mental discipline develops eye-control; eye-control indicates responsibilities. Once responsibilities are indicated the defensive man must follow them. This prevents the potential receiver from "sneaking up on" the pass defender and beating him on a long pass.

Eye-control also prevents "star-gazing" by the pass defenders. Star-gazing is watching the keys after they have established their direction. Once the keys have indicated direction there is no reason to watch them unless they are the responsibility of the defensive man who is doing the star-gazing. When direction is determined, the eyes must turn to the man for whom the pass defender is responsible—and give that offensive man complete attention. The coach, working behind the demonstrating team, can readily discern by the movement of the defender's eyes and head whether he is using proper eye-control.

Star-gazing can get the pass defender into serious trouble. While he continues to watch the keys longer than necessary, the potential receiver for whom he is responsible is running toward him with the intentions of beating him on a long pass. Every additional second the defender ignores the potential receiver for whom he is responsible and watches the offensive back—for whom he is *not* responsible—he is allowing the receiver to get closer and closer. When the potential receiver reaches a point three yards from the defender, it is too late; the offensive man has the defensive man licked. An effective pass defense will not include "star-gazers."

Playing pass defense and having run responsibilities puts a lot of pressure on the deep defenders. A mistake in the secondary can cost the team six points. Because of this ever-present fact it is stressed continually that the deep backs "stay honest." The pass defender must stay honest and take care of the man and the area he is responsible for before committing himself to help elsewhere. When an offensive end blocks, the defensive man responsible for him does not fire up to the line of scrimmage and leave him uncovered. He must stay with the end until the football, either in the ball carrier's arms or through the air, crosses the line of scrimmage. A blocking end does not release a secondary man of his responsibilities. We do not want a defensive back leaving his man quickly. He is told to take care of himself first, then help out his teammates.

We do not key ends for the reason outlined above and specifically because of what we saw Pete Pihos—the great pass-catching end of the Philadelphia *Eagles*—do. He blocked a defensive tackle beautifully—for three counts—all the while watching the defensive back. When the back reacted to the block by firing up to the line, Pete released from his block, ran downfield, and caught a touchdown pass.

Our secondary men are taught to key backs, to use eye-control, to pick up their respective responsibilities, and react to what their keys tell them. If the pass defender's responsibility is an end and he is blocking, then our pass defense man "lays off" and plays an area until the ball is thrown. Under no circumstances do we want the reaction of our pass defenders predicated upon the action of an offensive end.

We do not want our defensive backs making tackles on the line of scrimmage. Defensive backs cannot defend against passes and also stop the opponent's running game. They must be responsible for one or the other—not both. If the deep secondary backs are making a large number of tackles, the over-all defense is not fundamentally sound. Any time a deep halfback or safetyman makes a tackle on or within three yards of the line of scrimmage, he is courting trouble. That trouble will be forthcoming shortly in the form of a long pass—usually good for six points.

The deep back must defend against the pass first and the run second. Please do not get the idea that our backs do not tackle. They do—as witnessed by these facts: Sam Mudie (safety man) made 13 tackles against Princeton, Bob Yaksick (defensive halfback) got 14 tackles against Connecticut, and Pierce Frauenheim (defensive halfback) made 12 against Delaware. They tackle but *not on the line of scrimmage.*

A deep pass defender never should attempt to recover a fumble in the opponent's backfield. The defender does not have the remotest possibility of recovering the fumble so he should not attempt to get the ball. When a fumble occurs he must stay alert. Do not relax but do not attempt to recover the ball.

Regardless of what happens in the opponent's backfield, the secondary men must stay with potential receivers when they are coming downfield. This fundamental football truth was driven home very forcibly to me in the 1957 Pennsylvania-Princeton football game. The Princeton fullback fumbled the ball on their patented reverse pass. The Penn safety man reacted to the fumble, momentarily leaving the Princeton left end open. Their wingback continued on his reverse course, picked up the fumbled ball, stopped and threw the ball—alley-oop style—downfield to the waiting left end for a long and important pass completion. This completion led to Princeton's winning touchdown in a 13-9 defeat for Penn.

The deep defenders have a hard and fast rule

they can never break: *Number one is the pass— number two is the run.* They must always obey this rule.

Under our theory of defense, the linemen's responsibility is 100 percent against the running game; the linebackers' responsibilities are divided equally— 50 percent against the runs, 50 percent against passes. The deep secondary backs' responsibilities are 100 percent against passes.

Know What the Maze Is

The maze is a teaching aid. It is the area, laterally, between the offensive ends and, vertically, from the line of scrimmage to a point eight yards beyond the scrimmage line.

why not. 15 yards

The maze is diagramed in *Figure 8.* We have our groundskeeper lay out the maze on our practice field before fall practice begins so it will be ready for the opening day of drills. We continue to use it throughout fall practice. Pass defense practice always is conducted with the maze.

Using the maze develops a "sense of security" in the deep pass defenders regarding pass receivers in the eight-yard area, which lies directly in front of them. The deep defenders know that basically the maze is the linebackers' responsibility.

The linebackers must be cognizant of hook passes, crossing ends, delayed passes of all types, and backs circling in the maze. Linebackers must use their peripheral vision in this eight-yard area to combat passes. They must "feel" potential receivers coming into their territory and learn to bump them off stride.

Deep pass defenders do not commit quickly

THE MAZE

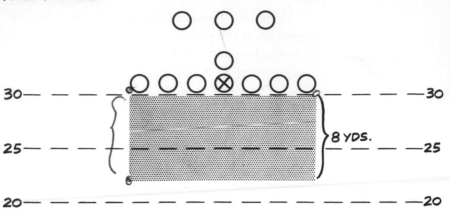

Figure 8

when a potential receiver is in the maze. Their primary responsibility is that receiver who passes through the maze and continues on a deep pass pattern. We want simultaneous tackles from our deep defenders on receivers catching hook passes in the maze. A hard, sure tackle many times causes the pass receiver to "turn the ball loose."

Utilizing the maze to build a feeling of security has nearly eliminated the effectiveness of the hook-and-go pass pattern against the pass defense.

The deep pass defenders know they have someone in front of them to help on short passes and the linebackers know they have the deep defenders who will help on any passes thrown in the eight-yard area known as the maze. This has strengthened our pass defense.

Ten Basic Principles of Our Pass Defense

Maintain Verbal Communication

Defensive backs must maintain direct voice contact with each other at all times. It is imperative that they talk to each other about: /

1. The tactical situation
2. Opponent's personnel (passer and receivers)
3. Their own responsibilities against any situation that can be anticipated

Only by maintaining verbal communication with each other will the pass defense gain cohesion and the ability to anticipate.

Talking to each other is particularly important when a crossing pattern is anticipated from two potential receivers. In our pass defense we call "switch" in certain situations against two receivers attempting a crossing pattern. Only the safetyman can call "switch"—but any back can and must call out a warning to his fellow pass defenders when a single receiver is establishing a crossing pattern. The warning system we use is described thus:

The defender from whose area the crossing receiver is leaving calls out his fellow defender's name and the word "crossing" into whatever area the potential receiver is going. If a potential receiver were crossing from Joe Kowalski's area to Pierce Frauenheim's territory Joe would call out: *"Pierce, crossing."* Once the crossing man has left the original area, that defender "stays at home," plays honest, and watches for any other eligible receiver coming across from the opposite direction. He does not go chasing across the field to help someone else and leave his own area unprotected until he has taken care of his own responsibilities first.

Once the ball crosses the line of scrimmage, either via the air or being carried, he then can release, fly to the ball, and help out his fellow defenders.

Cardinal Rule of Pass Defense:
No One Gets Behind Him, Ever

The cardinal rule of all pass defenders is never to let anyone get behind him. If a mistake is made—make it for depth. Under no circumstances, in no situation, can a defensive back let an offensive man get behind him.

Ten Basic Principles of Our Pass Defense

Three-Deep

Pass Defense Coverage

Chapter Five

THREE-DEEP (which in our terminology is called special) coverage is used primarily in our 53 defensive alignment but can also be used in our 54 and 61 alignments. Three-deep—special—coverage is the oldest and most fundamental type of pass defense coverage in football.

It is the easiest to teach and the easiest to learn because the three potential long receivers always belong to the three-deep secondary pass defenders. A linebacker or end, depending on the game called, has the second man out of the opponent's backfield. The pass defense assignments and responsibilities are clear-cut and precise. Using special coverage the pass defenders should have no doubts or hesitation.

Special coverage gets maximum coverage with a minimum of thinking. We keep it simple so that reaction is quick and positive.

Prior to teaching the three-deep alignment, we discuss it in detail with the pass defense men. A particular point is made of explaining its inherent strengths and weaknesses and also why the personnel are placed where they are in the special coverage. This gives the defensive men complete understanding of both the strong and weak aspects of the alignment, and enables them to play the defense intelligently.

This is done also with the pass defense aspects of each of the games that are taught and executed from the 53 defensive alignment. This is necessary because pass defense responsibilities vary with each different game used. It has been our experience that when a boy is aware of a definite weakness in the defense he is playing, he is quick to make the concerted effort necessary to compensate for the known weakness.

Our pass defense—as stated in Chapter Four—is built on a set of principles. Beginning with the most fundamental principles (alignment and stance) the principles are taught in progression.

Personnel Placement

Figure 9 shows our three-deep special alignment. The personnel are placed where they are for particular reasons. We place men on defense by offensive position rather than by individual skills. In the over-all plan of building a football team, offensive abilities take precedence over defensive skills; therefore a back is placed offensively first and defensively second. Our fullback plays middle line-

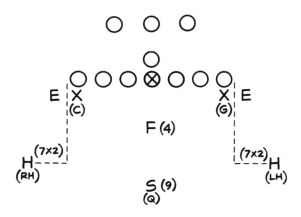

Figure 9: Alignment

Three-Deep Pass Defense Coverage

backer, the left halfback is the right defensive halfback, the right halfback plays left defensive halfback and the quarterback is our safetyman in the three-deep alignment. This is done for ease in training and substitution. We do not teach one quarterback the safety position and another the left defensive halfback simply because of a slightly greater aptitude for those positions.

Our fullback is the middle linebacker because he must be a heavy duty defensive man and has only secondary pass defense responsibilities. The center is placed to the opponent's right—where most teams prefer to run—because our centers are usually bigger than our guards, who are our other linebackers. Centers stand up better against the power of a concerted off-tackle running attack. Our guards, smaller and quicker, can cover passes, handle reverses, and react to screen passes better than the larger, less mobile center.

In the deep secondary, offensive quarterbacks are taught the safetyman's position. We do this because they should be, and usually are, the most knowledgeable football players on the squad. They must know our offense (especially all pass patterns) and other formations thoroughly. We capitalize on their training and ability by placing them at a strategic position on defense.

The offensive left halfback is placed at the right defensive halfback because he usually is the best and most versatile offensive back, possessing agility, quickness and good speed. He is placed where he is because he will be pitted against the players who are usually the opponent's prime receivers—their left ends.

This leaves the offensive right halfback playing

the left defensive halfback. Over the years, this position has provided us with some of our most consistent and best pass defenders. Most teams tend to set flankers to their right more than to the left, consequently the left defensive halfback must be a steady and alert pass defender because of the variety and complexity of the pass patterns that will run against him. Because of this, it is imperative that the left defensive halfback, above all other pass defenders, ignore fakes and not commit too fast.

Stance

Safetyman and all three linebackers use a parallel stance. They must be ready and able to move laterally in either direction, backward and forward.

The defensive halfbacks use a staggered stance with the outside leg back. Other than the foot position, all pass defense men are taught the same stance. Their knees are bent, ankles flexed, body and trunk lowered, shoulders forward, arms hanging loose (never do they anchor themselves to the ground by placing hands on knees), eyes focused on the offensive backs. Both mind and body must be keyed to a state of readiness. The pass defenders should not raise their heels off the ground—but they *should* be able to feel their toes in their shoes and be ready.

Identification of Opponent's Formation

It was stated in Chapter Four that the safetyman (quarterback) is responsible for identifying the opponent's offensive formation. It is not necessary to rediagram and identify all the formations again except to reiterate that correct formation identification is very important because the entire defense makes specific adjustments predicated on the safetyman's call.

Adjustments

The most important single aspect of pass defense is *proper position on the potential receiver,* both laterally and vertically.

In the adjustment rules we teach the pass defense personnel this fact is always paramount: the pass defender must always get and maintain good leverage on the potential receiver through proper position.

Figure 10 shows the adjustments that our entire defensive personnel make against specific formations.

In addition to over-all team adjustments, pass defense men are taught individual principles regarding adjustments.

Defensive halfbacks learn that they are always wider than widest potential receiver. They line up 7 yards deep and 2 yards outside the offensive end, or the widest potential receiver.

The safetyman aligns himself in the middle of the offensive formation and 9 yards deep. His lateral position will vary, of course, depending upon how wide the spread end or flanked back position themselves.

Deep secondary men are taught the six-yard sideline rule. This rule states that they never line up closer than six yards to the sideline. This gives the pass defender the leverage he wants when he is

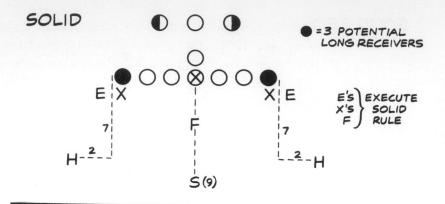

SOLID

● = 3 POTENTIAL LONG RECEIVERS

E's ⎫
X's ⎬ EXECUTE SOLID RULE
F ⎭

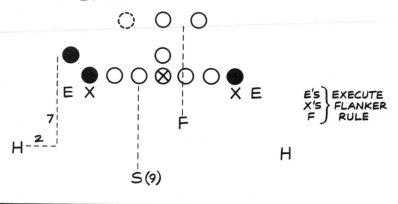

PEEL OR SPLIT

E's ⎫
X's ⎬ EXECUTE FLANKER RULE
F ⎭

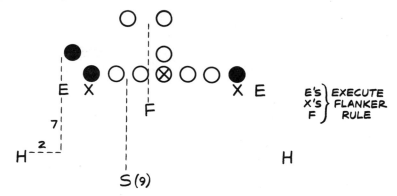

STRONG

E's ⎫
X's ⎬ EXECUTE FLANKER RULE
F ⎭

Figure 10: Against the double wing formation we automatically go to four-deep (box) coverage. We do not believe it is possible to cover four potential receivers with three pass defenders.

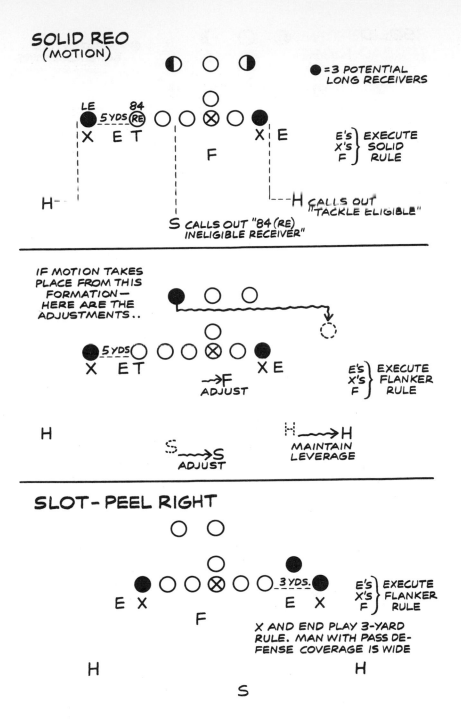

SOLID REO
(MOTION)

● = 3 POTENTIAL LONG RECEIVERS

LE 84
5YDS (RE)

X E T   F   X E

E's ⎫
X's ⎬ EXECUTE SOLID RULE
F ⎭

H

H CALLS OUT "TACKLE ELIGIBLE"

S CALLS OUT "84 (RE) INELIGIBLE RECEIVER"

IF MOTION TAKES PLACE FROM THIS FORMATION— HERE ARE THE ADJUSTMENTS..

5YDS

X E T   X E

→F
ADJUST

E's ⎫
X's ⎬ EXECUTE FLANKER RULE
F ⎭

H

S⟶S
ADJUST

H⟶H
MAINTAIN LEVERAGE

SLOT-PEEL RIGHT

E X   F   3 YDS. E X

E's ⎫
X's ⎬ EXECUTE FLANKER RULE
F ⎭

X AND END PLAY 3-YARD RULE. MAN WITH PASS DE-FENSE COVERAGE IS WIDE

H   H

S

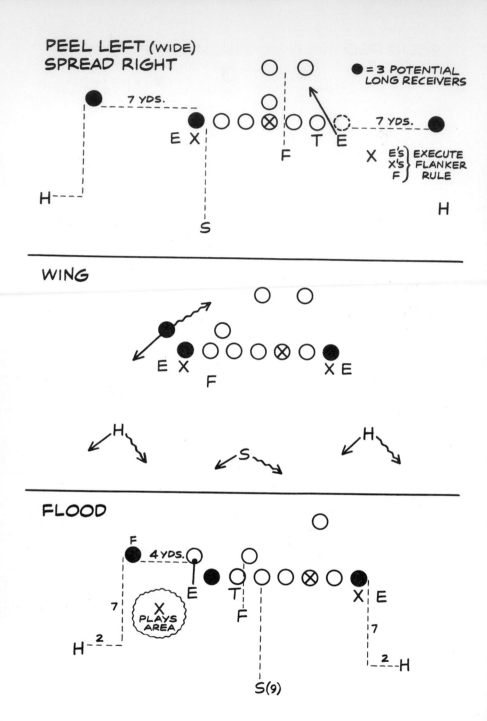

PEEL LEFT (WIDE)
SPREAD RIGHT

● = 3 POTENTIAL LONG RECEIVERS

7 YDS.

7 YDS.

E X

F

T E

X E's ⎫
   X's ⎬ EXECUTE FLANKER RULE
   F ⎭

H

S

H

WING

E X

F

X E

H

S

H

FLOOD

F

4 YDS.

E

T

F

X
PLAYS
AREA

7

H 2

T

X E

7

2 H

S(9)

playing the open side of the field. Using the six-yard sideline rule will sometimes put the pass defender in an inside-out position on the intended receiver. In this situation he uses the sideline to help him.

In all our adjustments we teach and expect the pass defenders to do some instinctive thinking.

Know the Three Potential Long Receivers

Once the opponent sets in his offensive formation, it is imperative that the deep secondary pass defenders determine the potential three long receivers. They are the three receivers who by reason of their offensive position can get downfield the quickest and consequently are the clear and present danger to the defense.

The three potential long receivers always belong to the three deep pass defenders. Knowing this instills a sense of security among the deep secondary men, because they know exactly for whom they are responsible.

The ends are two of the potential long receivers. The third will be determined by the offensive formation. If the opposition is aligned in a solid backfield the first man out of the backfield will be the third potential long receiver. If the offense is in a flanker formation then the flanker back becomes the third potential long receiver.

These three deep receivers always belong to the three deep secondary pass defenders. Any other receivers coming out of the backfield belong to linebackers or ends, depending upon the pass defense responsibilities specified in the game that has been called.

Following this principle eliminates any possibility of a defensive halfback thinking he covers the second man out of the backfield or a linebacker believing he is responsible for an end running a deep pass pattern. The only time a defensive halfback would cover the second man out of the offensive backfield is if one of the three potential long receivers did not come out for a pass. This relieves the deep man of his primary pass defense responsibility and now he can help cover the second man out on his side or a receiver crossing from the opposite side. The deep defender leaves his primary responsibility only after the ball has been thrown— never before.

Motion has come into football again in recent years. It has been the source of defensive problems just as it was in 1940 when the Chicago Bears exploded it on the football world. When the opponent uses motion we tell our defensive men to adjust, using this rule: *"What is the formation when the ball is snapped?"*

A solid backfield formation can become a peel, strong, or split formation depending on which back is in motion and in which direction he goes.

Our adjustments to motion are based on rules and the aforementioned principle that all pass defenders learn. We have found this approach to the motion problem satisfactory.

Know the Keys

Our keys (that determine flow) in special coverage are the offensive backs going in the same direction.

Against a solid backfield we can key for flow or

pre-determine. Doing this, we determine the formation strength before the ball is snapped and ignore flow. We pre-determine on a call by the safetyman. Against a flanker formation we will sometimes pre-determine and at times key for flow, depending upon the opposition's offense.

This method of keying gives us the flexibility we want and need in our pass defense coverage. Having this flexibility prohibits the opponent from dictating by formation, personnel or field position —to us what we must do in our three-deep coverage. They cannot force us into a particular coverage which they wish to exploit.

Develop Eye-Control and Know the Resulting Responsibilities

Developing eye-control in pass defense is very important. We devote a large amount of time to teaching this aspect of pass defense, as was pointed out in Chapter Four.

Through eye-control, the deep secondary men will move to their responsibilities once flow is established. The first move that our secondary pass defenders make, when flow is determined, is to go out at an angle, then back. It is necessary to move back but only after moving out first. The defensive back gives ground at an angle using the footwork maneuver. He should run in a manner that allows him to keep vision on the potential receiver while looking through him to the passer. This is known as *keeping leverage* on the intended receiver, and keeping good leverage on the receiver is constantly stressed.

Never should the pass defender make an inside

move first. When the defender moves back first and the potential receiver breaks out, the receiver will usually be open for the pass. For this reason we emphasize the importance of making a move to the outside at an angle first—then back.

When the potential receiver has made his first move downfield we stress, very strongly, that the pass defender keep his eye on the opponent's belt buckle while looking through him to the passer. Where the belt buckle of the adversary goes—he must go too!

Following the belt buckle eliminates the possibility of the defender being fooled by head, shoulder or eye fakes. While the intended receiver is going through his faking ritual, our pass defenders are taught to watch him, ignore his fakes and all the while keep dropping off, maintaining proper leverage on him. Doing this prevents any receiver from getting close enough to the defender to beat him on a long pass.

The potential receiver's intense efforts at faking prevent him from getting downfield for a long pass. A receiver in high school and college football seldom can do a good job of faking and also be sprinting downfield at full speed.

Pass Coverage Responsibilities vs. Solid Formation

Safetyman. When playing against a solid backfield formation the safetyman is responsible for the right end when flow goes right and the left end if flow goes left. His eyes must move to the right or left once his keys have moved two steps in the same direction and flow has been established.

Defensive halfbacks. Against a solid formation the defensive halfback is responsible for the end away from flow. When flow is toward him, he has first back out of the backfield. When flow is determined his eyes must immediately focus on the end or offensive halfback who is his responsibility.

Linebackers. Linebackers have important responsibilities in our pass defense coverage. Their ability can make the difference between weak, ordinary or good pass defense.

Contrary to what is taught the deep pass defenders, the linebackers watch the passer's eyes. They are close enough to the passer to see his eyes and perceive the direction that he intends to pass. We feel that the passer will throw where he looks.

Our middle linebackers, ends and outside linebackers have two rules regarding their pass coverage duties. One is a *Solid Rule* (for use against a solid formation), and the other is a *Flanker Rule* (to be used against flanker formations).

Establishing a set of rules concerning pass defense responsibilities has cut errors to a minimum. There is no guesswork; now it is a matter of getting good execution.

Middle linebacker. Our middle linebacker (fullback) lines up against a solid backfield, head-on and as deep as the offensive fullback. He has specific responsibilities against runs. When a pass shows, he follows his Solid Rule which says: "I cover the offensive fullback man-for-man. If he blocks, I drop off and cover the middle area in the maze."

Outside linebackers and ends. Our two outside linebackers (center and guard) and both ends have pass defense responsibilities in our 53 defensive alignment when special pass defense is called.

The end and linebacker playing alongside each other *never* have pass defense coverage duties simultaneously. The linebacker or the end has run responsibility in each game called. Whoever has run has no responsibilities for pass coverage. Whether they have run or pass responsibilities, they go first to their point of defensive responsibility then react to the ball. They must carry out their primary responsibility first! Their second—against passes—is next in importance!

Figure 11 shows some basic pass patterns from a solid backfield formation and what our pass defenders' reactions and responsibilities are, based on their Solid Rule, in our three-deep (special) pass defense coverage.

Pass Coverage Responsibilities Against Flanker Formation

When the opponents line up in a flanker formation, they immediately establish for us the three potential long receivers. This makes the deep pass defenders' job simpler.

Deep secondary defenders. The safetyman and defensive halfback on the side of the flanker are responsible for the flanker ·and the end closest to him. The defensive halfback must always be aware of his rule: *Line up as wide as the widest potential receiver.*

Safetyman and halfback toward flanker. Our safetyman and defensive halfback—who are responsible for the end-flanker combination—are taught three rules regarding their coverage against this two-man combination:

First, they must cover "long and short" on the

BASIC

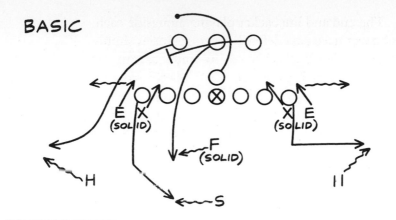

EAGLE

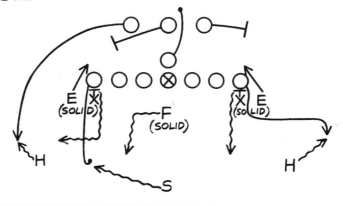

PINCH

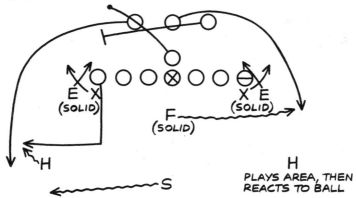

H
PLAYS AREA, THEN
REACTS TO BALL

Figure 11

BLITZ

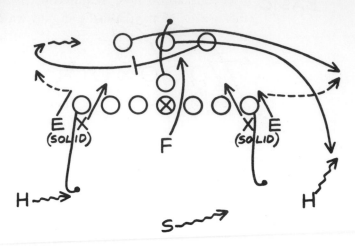

end-flanker combination. The defensive halfback covers the receiver who runs a short pass pattern, while the safetyman is responsible for the receiver who establishes a long pass pattern.

The second rule for coverage when playing against an end-flanker combination is the "inside-and-outside" principle. Our safety has the inside receiver of the two while the defensive halfback has the receiver who runs an outside pattern.

The third rule our two secondary pass defenders have is the "change-for-depth" principle. This is used when one receiver precedes the other by an appreciable distance or with greater speed. In this situation our two defenders are taught to go with the two men they are responsible for, playing them man-for-man, but anticipating a switch call. When "switch" is called, the deepest of the two defenders will assume responsibility for the deepest receiver. The other deep defender will cover the short receiver.

Three-Deep Pass Defense Coverage

This adjustment, required when the opponent sets a wide flanker, spreads an end wide, and sends one receiver down fast and the other delayed. In this situation it is most important that the deep defenders *do not* commit too quickly. It is better to stand still than to react too fast.

If a switch call is necessary, *only the safety-man* calls it. In effecting a switch the distance between receivers and comparative rates of speed must be considered. When both receivers come out at the same relative depth and width there is no problem. Deep pass defenders must see potential receivers coming into their areas without more than a glance at them. They can thus anticipate a switch and be ready to react when it is called.

In our theory of pass defense, a specific defender is responsible *immediately* for each potential receiver. He is charged with that responsibility until the ball is passed or until someone else assumes responsibility for him. This can happen on a switch call by the safetyman. We do not turn a man loose when a potential receiver leaves an area. We do not change responsibilities in mid-stream just because the potential receiver has passed through a certain area or crossed an imaginary line. We want specific defensive responsibilities for each offensive pass receiver at all times. Another pass defender must pick up the intended receiver and call out, "I have 87, Joe," then assume the responsibility of covering him, before the original defender is released of his responsibility.

Defensive halfback away from flanker. The defensive halfback away from the end-flanker combination covers the end on his side man-for-man. His job is to maintain outside leverage on the end and cover him wherever he goes. If his end spreads wide, our linebacker will make an adjustment and the defensive halfback will have help in covering him. Should the end cross shallow, in the maze, the defensive halfback will follow his rule regarding crossing ends (as discussed in Chapter Four).

If the opponent should line up in a flanker (end-back) formation and then put the flanker man in motion back across the offensive formation between the line of scrimmage and the offensive backs, we would follow our motion rule: *"What is the formation when the ball is snapped?"*—and play it accordingly.

Another point concerning the responsibilities of the three-deep secondary men against passes. They must learn to diagnose quickly whether a potential receiver is attempting to run a deep or short pass pattern. This is readily discernible by watching closely the first four steps the receiver takes. A player going deep will show this immediately by the quickness with which he gets away from the line of scrimmage. A short receiver usually will not fire out from his offensive stance but will go at half-speed to set up the proper timing on the pass pattern. These points are important for deep pass defenders to know.

It is also necessary for deep secondary defenders to know the personnel they are playing against. They must know whether the left end is a 5' 10", 175-pound speedster and if the right end is a 6' 2", 210-pound tackle-type end. It makes a difference. Pass defenders play various receivers in different ways depending upon size, speed and type. The smaller end will be played as a long receiver

while the bigger end will be treated as a short receiver and be watched for button-hook, square-out
and crossing patterns. Considerable time is spent
discussing personnel in practice on Monday night.
(This is covered in Chapter Eight, which is devoted
to pass defense practice planning.)

Middle linebackers. Against a flanker formation, the middle linebacker (fullback) lines up
midway between the two backs remaining in the
opponent's backfield, and four yards deep. From
this vantage point he carries out his responsibilities
against runs. Against passes, he follows his Flanker
Rule which is: "I take the first of the two remaining
backs; if they divide or cross—I take the halfback."
If neither of the backs goes out for a pass, the
middle linebacker drops back, covering the middle
territory. Following this rule, we sometimes will
end up with double coverage on a receiver but
this is not disastrous. A verbal signal is used to release one defender to other duties.

Outside linebackers and ends. When we
face a flanker formation and the opponent attempts
a pass, our outside linebackers and ends follow the
Flanker Rule. This rule states: "I take the second
of the two remaining backs. If he does not come,
I drop to my hook area or play the short flat—depending on the situation." Against runs, they go
to their points of defensive responsibility dictated
by the game that has been called.

In our 53 defensive alignment, linebackers and
ends are taught principles which they follow in ad-
justing to spread ends and flankered backs.

If an end spreads more than three yards, our
linebackers and ends will adjust to an equidistant
position. (This position was discussed in Chapter

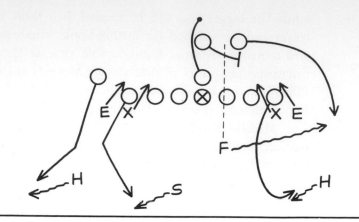

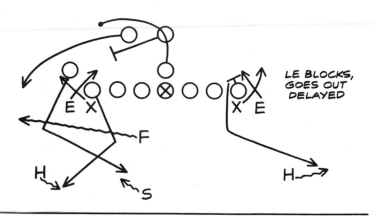

LE BLOCKS,
GOES OUT
DELAYED

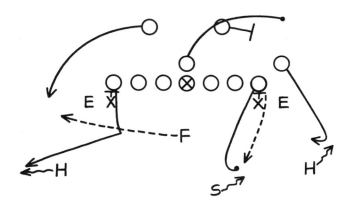

Figure 12

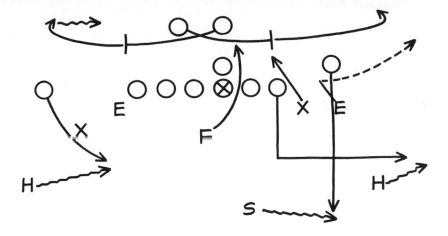

Four.) The linebacker or end who has pass defense responsibilities in the game called will be the equidistance man. We want our linebackers assuming this responsibility 90 percent of the time. They keep their same responsibilities against runs and passes but from the equidistance position.

Figure 12 shows flanker formations with different backfield maneuvers and pass defenders' responsibilities, based on our Flanker Rule in our three-deep (special) pass defense coverage.

In three-deep (special) coverage it is particularly important to stress the significance of the maze. The area most vulnerable to exploitation in three-deep coverage is the short flat territory in front of the defensive halfbacks. It is the linebacker's duty to help out in this area. We do not want our halfbacks unduly concerned about this short area and making tackles on the line of scrimmage.

The Responsibilities of the Deep Secondary Against Runs

The final portion of this chapter will be devoted to the responsibilities the three-deep secondary men have against the running game.

The three men are assigned specific patterns of approach when coming up to meet a ball carrier with blockers preceding him.

Figure 13 shows the routes the defensive halfbacks and safetymen are taught to follow when meeting a running play.

First, the deep secondary must establish the fact that the play is definitely a run. This is done by watching the correct keys, checking the action of the offensive backs, and following our eye-control rules to see what the potential receivers are doing. After doing this, if there are any remaining doubts they must play the pass first and run second.

Defensive halfbacks. When the defensive halfback is attacked by a running play, he approaches the play but keeps himself *wider than the widest man* (be he blocker or ball carrier) coming out of the opponent's backfield. When coming up to make the tackle, the halfback should be aggressive but under control. His job is to turn the play in or make the tackle from the outside. He *never* allows the ball carrier to get outside of him. The defensive halfback takes care of his territory first, then helps his fellow defensive backs.

When the play goes away from the halfback, he becomes a conservative halfback. He does not chase wildly and attempt to make the tackle across the field. When the play is definitely going away from him, the defensive halfback moves to the area

Three-Deep Pass Defense Coverage

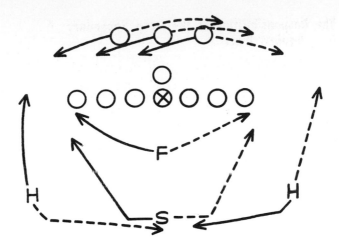

Figure 13

vacated by the safetyman. He plays football from there, watching for trick plays, naked reverses, transcontinental (across field) passes, and delayed plays of any type.

Safetyman. The safetyman—when the play is definitely established as a run—moves laterally in the same direction that the ball is going.

He moves as fast as the ball but a step behind. When the ball carrier turns upfield, the safetyman approaches him from an inside-out course at a 45 degree angle on a straight line. The safetyman is responsible for any cut-backs by the ball carrier and must never over-run the ball.

He takes care of his own territory first and only on long runs should he ever be forced to make tackles across the field. His job is to prevent touchdowns—not first downs.

The safetyman's approach to the ball carrier in

the open field is a conservative one—slide, jockey for position and, if need be, retreat. He delays the runner's advance until help comes from teammates. He makes use of the sidelines.

The safetyman must always be under control. He approaches the ball carrier conservatively and makes tackles with confidence.

Three-Deep Pass Defense Coverage

Four-Deep

Pass Defense Coverage

Chapter Six

IN our football nomenclature, four-deep pass defense is called "box" coverage. The word is descriptive, easily enunciated and easily understood.

Box coverage is used in both our 54 and 61 defensive alignments. Having both three-deep and four-deep coverage allows us theoretically—to cover any pass pattern in football. We feel they are both necessary to a complete pass defense.

Four-deep coverage came into being because teams could not adequately cover the double hook (ends) and double swing (halfbacks) pass patterns. Box coverage can do this. Also, as stated in Chapter Five, I do not believe that three-deep pass defenders can cover four potential receivers, which the double wing formation forces the defense to do. We want four defenders in position to cover four possible receivers—all of whom could be long receivers. Box coverage provides us with the answer to this problem.

In our box coverage—contrary to what many football teams do—we do not always rotate into three-deep coverage on movement of the ball. Whether we do or do not rotate depends upon the offensive formation we face and also the action of the backs in that particular formation. If we were always rotating into three-deep from four-deep, then teaching box coverage would be unnecessary and a waste of time—because we already have three-deep coverage. We want the ability to cover the "four men out" patterns, and that is what our box coverage gives us.

As is true with three-deep (special) coverage, there are certain inherent strengths and weaknesses in box coverage also. These are discussed in detail with the pass defense men prior to teaching the four-deep alignment. Particularly is this done with each of the games that are used in the 54 and 61 defensive alignments. This provides the defensive men with understanding concerning the 54 and 61 defenses and the box secondary coverage.

As stated in Chapter Four we build our pass defense on a set of principles. Principles are taught rather than situations, because with the great number of formations used in modern football, we find it impossible to prepare for each formation individually. Using a set of principles has helped us in alleviating the problem of preparing for many and varied formations. We feel it is mandatory to have "operating principles" for good pass defense.

In box coverage the first principle we teach is *Alignment and Stance*.

SOLID

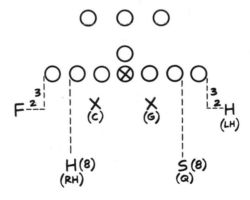

Figure 14

Personnel Placement

Figure 14 shows our four-deep (box) alignment. For terminology we refer to the two corner men as corner linebackers, the deep men as safetymen and the two linebackers lined up on the offensive guards are inside linebackers.

Our offensive left halfbacks play the right corner linebacker position and the fullbacks are the left corner linebackers. Our offensive quarterbacks are the right safetymen; the offensive right halfbacks play the left safety position. Further details regarding their positions against various formations will be discussed under adjustments later in this chapter. Our center and guard are the two inside linebackers in our 54 defensive alignment, while in the 61 alignment the guard goes into the line and the center becomes the middle linebacker.

In Chapter Five it was explained why players in certain offensive positions are assigned to particular defensive positions in our three-deep secondary. They stay fundamentally the same in our four-deep secondary alignment. We placed the personnel where we did because most football teams are "right-handed" when both running and passing. Placing our four-deep men as we do, we will end up, when the opponent runs or passes to his right (our left), with the same three pass defenders playing deep as in our three-deep (special) coverage. Placing the men in these positions has eliminated the necessity of double-learning and as a result it has helped us.

The success of the 54 defensive alignment, whether operating against runs or passes, is dependent upon good linebackers. It is appropriate therefore to discuss here the requisites that the inside and outside linebackers should possess to make the defense effective.

The inside linebackers must be the stronger, heavier men of the four linebackers. They are combination linebackers and linemen who must be able to back up the line, delay potential receivers, rush the passer, stop the off-tackle play, drop off into the hook area and also cover the fullback on "swing" and screen passes.

Corner linebackers must be a combination of defensive ends and deep halfbacks. Against runs they must be "tough-nosed" ends, but when playing against passes they must be "nimble" pass defenders. They must possess both maneuverability and toughness. Needless to say, good corner linebackers are very rare and difficult to find in high school and college football. We were fortunate at Rutgers, in our 1961 undefeated season, to have two boys—Bob Yaksick and Joe Kowalski—who were particularly adept at playing this difficult position.

Stance

All four-deep (box) defense men are taught the same fundamental stance, except for foot position. Their knees are bent, ankles flexed, body and trunk lowered, shoulders forward, arms hanging loose (never do they anchor themselves to the ground by putting their hands on their knees), and their eyes are focussed on the offensive backs. They must be ready to move instantly.

The two corner linebackers use a staggered stance with the outside leg back. Their bodies are

Four-Deep Pass Defense Coverage

cocked slightly to the inside. They line up, against a solid backfield, three yards deep and two yards outside of the offensive ends, or the widest potential receiver.

Both safetymen use a parallel stance; they line up, against a solid backfield, on the outside shoulders of the offensive tackles at a depth of eight yards.

The two inside linebackers also use a parallel stance and line up, against a balanced line, head-on with the offensive guards, one and one-half yards behind the line of scrimmage.

Regardless of alignment or stance, all pass defenders must keep their minds and bodies alert.

Identification of Opponent's Formation

As stated in Chapter Four, correct identification of the opponent's formations by the safetyman is very important. Particularly is this true when using box coverage because of the multiplicity of adjustment to be made. Consequently, the safetyman must be thinking alertly at all times.

The importance of correct calls must be emphasized because we make certain defensive adjustments against each specific formation used by the opposition.

Adjustments

Proper position, both laterally and vertically, on the potential receiver is a "must" for playing good pass defense. A football player cannot be a good pass defender unless he has the correct position on the intended receiver both *before* and *after* the ball is passed. With this ever-present reality in mind

we spend considerable time teaching all those involved in pass defense the adjustments to correct
position they must make before the ball is thrown.
We emphasize this point, because we have found
that the pass defender will usually be in the proper
position *after* the ball is thrown too. Good leverage
by the pass defender must always be maintained on
the intended receiver. Adjustment to correct position helps to get leverage and hold it.

In Chapter Five we emphasized the importance of pass defenders having individual principles
regarding pass coverage, in addition to the principles
governing over-all pass defense. These individual
principles include such things as the six-yard sideline
rule, the safetyman always lining up in the middle
of the offensive formation, and the "wide-as-the-
widest-potential-receiver" rule that halfbacks and
corner linebackers must obey. These principles also
apply in box coverage.

Figure 15 shows the adjustments our defensive
personnel make against the peel, split and wing formations from our four-deep (box) secondary alignment.

When playing against peel, split or wing formations we cock our four-deep backs toward the
flanker and play flow. Most teams using these formations tend to run toward the flanker. If they do,
by cocking our backs, we can complete our rotation
quickly and be in good position to defend against
the pass or run. By cocking our backs, we are also
in good position when they run away from the
flanker back. From this position, we can play flow,
then move back and across to meet the offensive
maneuver that is being directed at us—be it pass or
run.

Four-Deep Pass Defense Coverage

PEEL

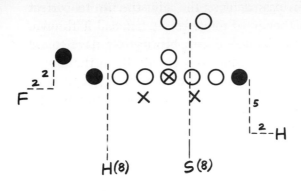

SPLIT

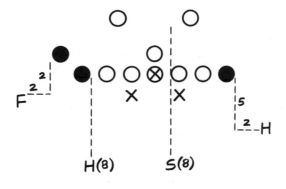

WING

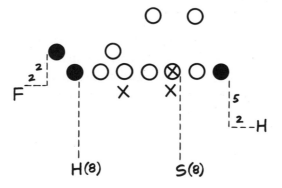

Figure 15

If an opponent directs a greater portion of his offense to the flanker and runs little or no offense away from him, we can play the formation as a "strong" one and rotate to the flanker. This gives us flexibility in our adjustments against all offensive formations.

When the flanker back sets wide (four yards or more from his end), the corner linebacker nearest the flanker back goes out with him, maintaining his correct leverage on the flanker. The nearest safetyman also adjusts to a position midway between thc flanker back (the widest potential receiver) and the nearest possible receiver to the flanked back.

Figure 16 shows our adjustment against both a "strong" and a "flood" formation.

In our box coverage, when playing against the strong and/or flood formations, we rotate the four deep backs to the flanker back and pre-determine.

It has been our experience that these two offensive formations are used primarily when a team seeks to establish a running attack. We meet their power with our power—by doing a complete rotation to the flanker back.

If a team directs their attack away from the flanker back we are in position to defend against their running plays and passes. If a major part of their offense is directed away from the flanker back then we can play the formation as a *peel-and-cock* rather than rotate.

When the flanker is positioned wide (four yards or more from the end), our corner linebacker to the side of the flanker will rotate and place himself in an equidistant position. The equidistant position was discussed in Chapter Four. The inset drawing in *Figure* 16 shows where the equidistant man lines up when the flanker is wide.

Four-Deep Pass Defense Coverage

STRONG

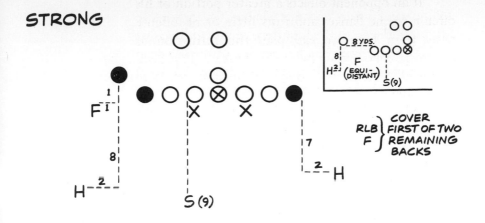

COVER
RLB } FIRST OF TWO
F } REMAINING
BACKS

FLOOD

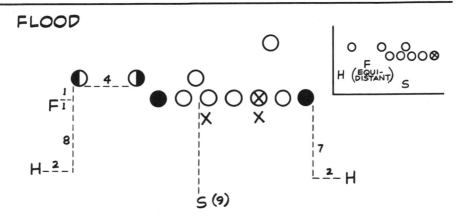

Figure 16

When we play against the double wing formation our deep secondary men will adjust as they do
against a solid backfield. The backs place themselves in a balanced alignment, since the offense can
go either right or left equally well.

Figure 17 shows our alignment against the

Four-Deep Pass Defense Coverage

double wing formation from our box coverage. We automatically go to the four-deep alignment against a double wing formation because we want four-deep pass defenders in position to cover four potential long receivers when the ball is snapped.

Spread ends have come into football recently to plague the over-all defense and pass defense in particular. *Figure 18* shows two adjustments our defensive personnel are taught to make against them.

The purpose of these adjustments is to take away the diagonal pass to the spread end and also to be in position to cover the offensive left halfback on a swing or circle and square-out pass pattern.

We accomplish these objectives in two ways. One, we "invert" our inside safety to the side of the spread end. When a safety inverts, the corner linebacker, next to him, drops off to his special coverage position. Two, we move the defensive end and tackle, on the side of the spread end, in one man and station the near linebacker in an equidistant position. From here, we play our box coverage pass defense principles.

Figure 19 shows what we do against motion from our four-deep (box) coverage. As in special coverage, we follow our motion rule—"What is the formation when the ball is snapped?" Adhering to our pass defense principles will put us in the proper position both before and after the ball is snapped, with or without "motion."

Against the original peel formation (in Figure 19) the backs would cock and play flow. When motion comes they follow their principles and react accordingly.

The offensive formation in *Figure 20* has given the defense considerable trouble since the mid-

DOUBLE WING

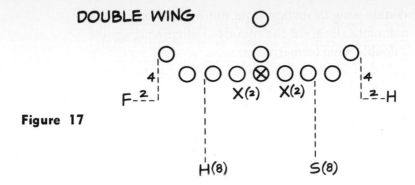

Figure 17

SPREAD RIGHT

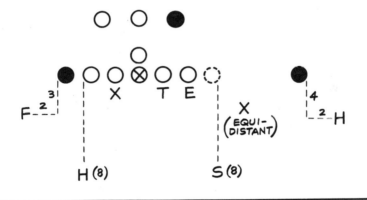

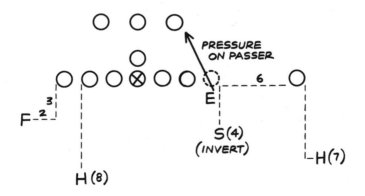

Figure 18

1950's when Eddie Erdelatz used it so successfully during his coaching tenure at the United States Naval Academy. At that time the author was Steve Sebo's backfield coach at the University of Pennsylvania. Navy was on our schedule and we had to defense this formation—sometimes not too successfully—but in 1959 we tied Navy 22 to 22 and the two adjustments shown proved to be effective against this formation. It is essentially a passing formation and as such is discussed here.

Know the Potential Long Receivers

The four deep pass defenders in box coverage must always know the potential long receivers. A great percentage of the time there will be three long receivers but sometimes there will be four—all of whom belong to the four deep men charged with pass defense responsibilities.

The four potential long receivers are quickly recognized when playing against a solid backfield, and the halfbacks divide then go on pass patterns while the ends also go out as pass receivers. This is true also when the opposition is using the double wing formation.

When the defense is playing against a flanker formation, the action of the remaining halfback (away from the flanker) will tell the pass defender whether there will be three or four possible long receivers. When the remaining back goes away from the flanker there could be four potential long receivers. If he goes toward the flanker, there will be three receivers who can get deep.

If flow takes place to the right or left in a solid or double wing formation, the rotating pass de-

Four-Deep Pass Defense Coverage

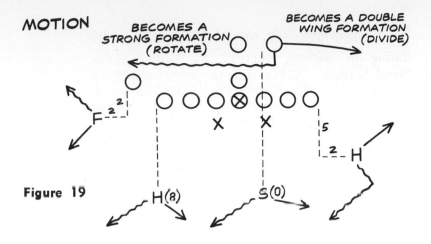

Figure 19

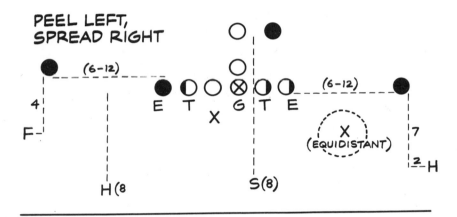

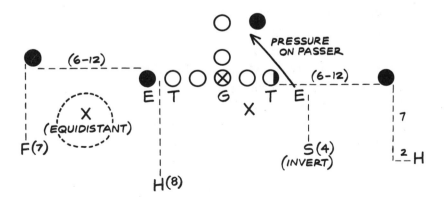

Figure 20

fenders must determine quickly the potential long receivers—because they are *immediately* responsible and must cover them.

This principle, concerning the potential long receivers, was discussed in Chapter Four and also in Chapter Five in regard to our three-deep (special) coverage, where it is particularly important that the three-deep pass defense men are able to spot the potential long receivers. Since we rotate at times from four-deep to three-deep in our box coverage, it is equally important that the four deep pass defenders know which four receivers can get downfield the quickest, by reason of their offensive position.

Regardless of what formation the pass defense men face—be it a regular or an "odd-ball" offensive set-up—they will be successful as long as they keep their poise, determine who the potential long receivers are, then achieve and maintain proper position on them.

Keys

It is my conviction that synchronized group movement can be correctly executed only by having all four deep pass defenders reacting to the same key. They must move together and simultaneously, for this reason our keys, for the four deep pass defense men, in box coverage are the offensive backs. We key them 100 percent.

Keys vs. solid formations. If the offense is aligned in a solid backfield formation, the halfbacks will tell us whether we react to flow and move right or left to the three-deep alignment or whether we stay in four-deep.

We do not always rotate to three-deep when using box coverage. There are times when we play four-deep all the way. The action of the offensive backs will determine for us whom we will cover.

When the offensive halfbacks cross or divide (go in opposite directions) we do not flow out but stay in four-deep coverage. If they move to the right or left we flow into a three-deep alignment by using our box coverage keys. We assume our responsibilities from our new positions. We flow from the four-deep to the three-deep alignment—but do not use special coverage keys. We end up showing a three-deep alignment but are covering by four-deep keys.

For a change-up we also use a pure zone coverage from within the framework of our four-deep secondary alignment. We get this by calling a signal. This will be discussed later in this chapter.

The keys for the inside linebackers against a solid backfield formation are very simple. They key the fullback (for whom they are responsible 100 percent) and watch the passers' eyes for direction.

Keys vs. flanker formations. When playing against flanker formations, while using our four-deep box coverage we will cock and play flow against peel, split, and wing formations. When we do this our key is the remaining halfback (away from the flanker back). If, when using our box coverage, we play against a strong or flood formation we will do a complete rotation to the flanker back and predetermine. When this is done, we ignore flow and play the formation with a three-deep secondary alignment.

We have two methods of rotating. One is the complete rotation toward the flanker back by the four-deep backs. This rotation can be to the right or left depending on the position of the flanker back. The weakness of this adjustment is that if we are forced to rotate to the right, we must teach all four men new positions and we also end up with our fullback being a three-deep halfback. This is fine occasionally, but not down after down. The second method of rotating is to make the fullback (left corner linebacker) a rover and always place him to the side of the flanker. He learns the position thoroughly. Using this method keeps the three secondary men constant and the same player always plays to the side of the flanker back. We use the latter adjustment when playing a team which uses a strong left (offensive) formation most of the time.

There are also situations when we play a strong formation and key for flow, thereby not pre-determining. We do this when two conditions prevail:

1. A team runs a large part of the offense away from the flanker back.
2. We have a left corner linebacker who can line up on the flanker back 1 yard directly in front of and 1 yard to the outside of him; he can cover the flanker deep when flow goes away.

Our Penn Team did this against Harvard in 1959 when they ran most of their offense away from the flanker. Jack Hanlon was an exceptional corner linebacker who could handle such a difficult assignment.

Let me reiterate that in our system of pass defense we learn basic principles of operation, then can and do deviate from them. For instance, basically we play a solid formation with a balanced secondary, a peel formation with a cocked secondary, and strong formation with a rotated secondary—but on a verbal command we can and do play the strong formation with a cocked secondary, the peel with a rotated secondary, then we will sometimes play the double wing with flow. All this is done depending on the type of offense the opponent uses from a specific formation. Having this flexibility prevents any team from setting us in a pass defense adjustment and proceeding to take us apart. We do not want this to happen!

Eye-Control and Responsibilities

The degree of importance we put on eye-control was previously discussed in Chapter Five. It is so important that we think a strong pass defense cannot be built unless it is emphasized and continually drilled.

Proper eye-control interprets flow and the subsequent coverage responsibilities. Obeying eye-control puts the defender in a good leverage position on the potential receiver which is the secret to effective pass defense. Consequently, we believe in developing eye-control.

Pass Coverage Responsibilities

Good linebackers are a requisite to the success of the 54 defensive alignment and four-deep (box) pass defense coverage. No team using either the 54 or 61 alignment can be successful unless it has good football players at these four vital positions. The defense requires linebackers to assume and to execute many responsibilities, both against the running game and passes.

Corner linebackers. *When flow is toward them . . .*

First the corner linebacker must know the defensive game that is being played. Particularly he must know what his own end (nearest him) is doing. (Our ends have no pass defense coverage responsibilities in the 54 or 61 defensive alignments.)

With the flow coming toward them the corner linebacker comes up to the line of scrimmage, always maintaining the two-yard gap between himself and the end man on the line. He plays the line of scrimmage and does not "bury" himself in the opponent's backfield, remembering that the end, tackle or inside linebacker—depending on the game called—is responsible for containment.

When a pass play is evident, the corner linebacker drops off the line of scrimmage at a 45 degree angle to his outside and covers the short area (to a depth of four yards) off the scrimmage line. He covers any receivers coming into the four yard zone; if the receiver (usually the near halfback) goes three or four yards behind him, the corner linebacker plays in front of him. When the ball is thrown he extends his arms high above his head, forcing the passer to throw through and over him to complete the pass. When flow is toward the corner linebacker and the near offensive halfback runs a swing pattern then continues deep (going through the short four-yard area), the corner man is *not* responsible The safetyman must cover him. The linebacker must be aware of the near end running a square-out pattern, the far end coming across in his area, or the fullback coming his direction.

If no receivers show, the linebacker defends the

four-yard area and reacts to the ball when it is passed.

When flow is away from them . . .

When flow is away from the corner linebacker, he drops off the line of scrimmage immediately— using his footwork maneuver—at a 45 degree angle, keeping leverage on the near end. As he is dropping off the line, he looks through the near end to the backfield and passer. The corner linebacker is responsible for the near end whether he runs a deep flag pattern, a quick bootleg, or a deep crossing pass route. He must be particularly cognizant of the bootleg pass.

While dropping off at a 45 degree angle, the corner man *cannot* turn inside. Most boys playing this position have a tendency to do this. It can be disastrous because he can be easily beaten to his outside by a smart receiver.

A strong point to stress with corner linebackers is this: they cannot cross the middle of the offensive formation until the ball crosses the line of scrimmage, when flow is away from them. Following this rule will prevent the completion of the bootleg and crossing pass patterns.

Safetymen. *When flow is toward them . . .*

When flow is toward the safetyman he rotates to the outside—in the direction of flow—getting outside leverage on the potential receiver. His coverage assignment is the deep outside area with specific responsibilities; usually the near end or halfback. Eye-control will take the safetyman to the man for whom he is responsible. Basically, he and the other safetymen have the offensive end and halfback to the side of flow. They play them "long and short," "inside and outside," and are watching for a switch situation between the two receivers (end and half-back).

When flow is away from them . . .

The safetyman, when flow is away from him, moves to the inside, getting depth and covering the deep middle area. He is now the middle safetyman and must be a "bastion of defense." His eye-control will take him to the end for whom he is responsible on most passes. This pass defender must positively play everything for a pass—until the run is definitely established. This man more than any other pass defender must never be faked out of position by the passer making a false move or fakes by the receivers. He gives his complete attention to the potential receiver—then reacts to the ball *only* after it leaves the passer's hands.

Inside linebackers. The inside linebackers' prime responsibility is never to allow themselves to be blocked to the inside. They go to their point of defensive responsibility—which the game they are executing calls for—*then* they react to the pass when it is indicated, but only after completing their assignment against the running play.

When the inside linebackers have gone to their run responsibilities and a pass is indicated, they then drop back to cover in their maze area, all the while maintaining good body balance. The inside

Four-Deep Pass Defense Coverage

linebackers must be more aware of the maze and its importance in box coverage because their duties and responsibilities are greater. They are responsible for the eight-yard area back of the line of scrimmage between the offensive ends.

When an inside linebacker goes to his hook point or pass defense responsibilities, he should not go until the passer goes by the two remaining backs who are his protectors. This eliminates the threat of a draw play.

When dropping to their hook points, inside the maze, inside linebackers must keep vision on the passer (watch his eyes), never turning their backs or losing sight of the passer. They key the offensive fullback because he is the man for whom they are responsible. If he goes to his own left, our right inside linebacker covers him. When the fullback goes to his own right, our left inside linebacker is responsible for him. (In our 61 defensive alignment, the middle linebacker covers the fullback man-for-man.)

Inside linebackers must never allow *any* eligible receivers to cross in front of them. Using their peripheral vision, they must be able to see an end or back—without looking directly at him—coming across in front of them and attempting to get to the other side of the field. When the inside linebacker sees this happening, he must make sure that the potential receiver is forced to go behind him.

If the intended receiver attempts to cross in front of him, the inside linebacker must step up and deliver a forearm blow into the receiver. This should knock him down or destroy the timing of his effort to get across the field. If the potential receiver attempts to cross behind him, the linebacker should drop back forcing the receiver to go behind him to get across the field.

Figure 21 is a solid backfield formation with pass patterns showing flow going both toward and

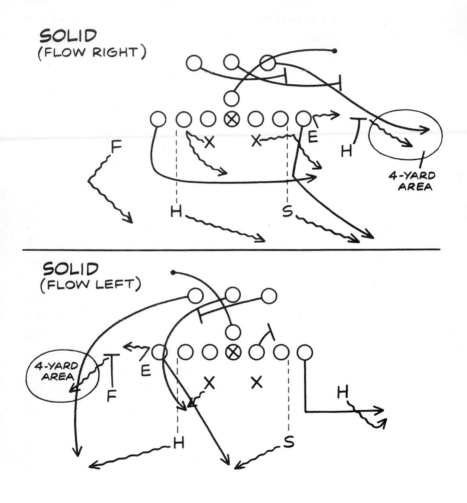

Figure 21

Four-Deep Pass Defense Coverage

away from the corner linebackers and safetymen. It shows our pass defenders reacting to flow and the responsibilities they assume from four-deep (box) coverage. The next figure (22) shows a flanker formation with the back that we key going toward the flanker—which also determines flow (see page 152).

We have covered reactions and responsibilities of the four deep men in box coverage when flow is toward or away from them. In addition there are situations against both solid and flanker formations when flow will not take place. This happens in the solid and wing formation when the two halfbacks— whom we are keying—go in opposite directions (divide) or cross. We call and play this maneuver as a divide pass pattern. When it takes place our four deep pass defenders will drop off, staying in their box coverage, not rotating, and watching the offensive near end and near halfback. The corner linebackers and safeties play "inside-outside," "long and short," and watch for a switch situation by the two potential receivers on their side.

The divide pass pattern with the resulting action and coverage responsibilities can also follow from a peel and split formation. This happens when the remaining halfback goes away from the flanker. If the remaining halfback moves *toward* the flanker we continue our rotation from the cocked position and will cover an ensuing pass from a three-deep alignment. To get this reaction (rotation) from our deep backs, the remaining offensive halfback must make a *definite move toward* the flanker. If he dives into the line, blocks or just stands still, we play it as a divide pattern—because he is still a possible fourth deep receiver.

Figure 23 shows our box coverage pass de-

PEEL
(FLOW TO FLANKER)

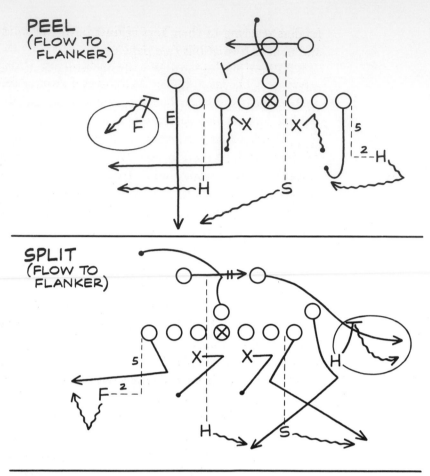

SPLIT
(FLOW TO FLANKER)

WING
(FLOW TO FLANKER)

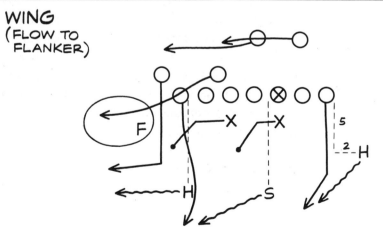

Figure 22

fenders reacting to their keys against both the solid and flanker formations *(see page 154)*.

When playing against a strong formation, we rotate to the flanker most of the time. Consequently, we would never be put in the position of having to cover a divide pass pattern when in a complete rotation against the strong formation. *Figure 24* shows how we would cover passes where the remaining backs go both toward and away from the flanker. If we found it necessary to cover a large number of passes similiar to the second pass, we would play the strong formation as a peel, cock to it and play flow.

Whenever we play against the double wing formation we use box coverage against it. If we are not in a four-deep alignment at the time, we go automatically to it. The pass defenders are taught that a double wing formation is the same as a solid backfield with the halfbacks already in a divide pattern—so we still key the halfbacks in the double wing formation.

If both halfbacks go out on pass routes, along with the ends, we play it the same as a divide pattern from a solid formation. When either of the two halfbacks, in the double wing, goes into motion back across the offensive formation, we move with them and rotate into three-deep (special) coverage.

Figure 25 shows our reactions against the double wing. The first part is a divide pass pattern, while the second shows a halfback in motion and how our pass defenders react to this *(see page 157)*.

Earlier in this chapter *(see page 143)* reference was made to a "change-up coverage" we use from our four-deep alignment; that is a true four-deep zone.

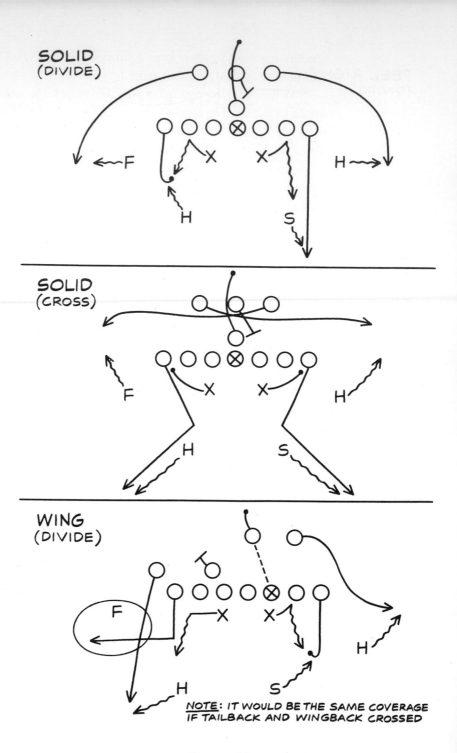

SOLID
(DIVIDE)

SOLID
(CROSS)

WING
(DIVIDE)

NOTE: IT WOULD BE THE SAME COVERAGE IF TAILBACK AND WINGBACK CROSSED

Figure 23

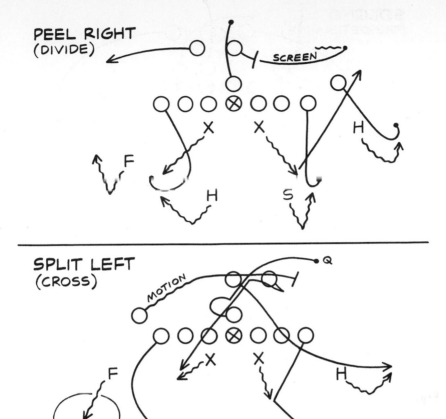

PEEL RIGHT
(DIVIDE)

SCREEN

SPLIT LEFT
(CROSS)

MOTION

Q

AREA

This is the third type of pass defense coverage that was referred to in Chapter One, dealing with our philosophy of multiple defense.

We get the true four-deep zone coverage from our box coverage alignment by adding the word *set* to the original word *box*. When the *box-set* coverage is used, the four-deep pass defense men divide

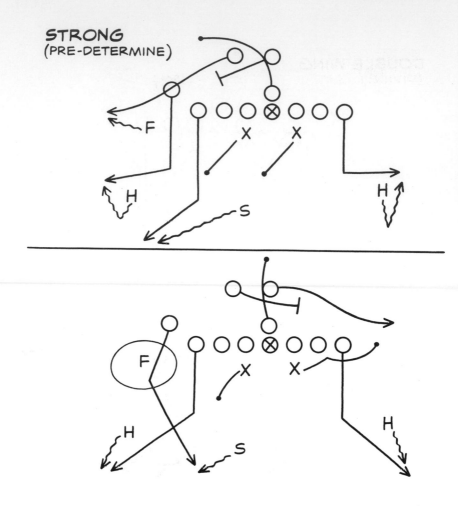

Figure 24

the football field into four quarters (areas). Each is responsible for an area, has specific responsibilities, and plays the ball when it is thrown. The keys for the four-deep men in box-set coverage are the near back and the near end.

Four-Deep Pass Defense Coverage

DOUBLE WING
(DIVIDE)

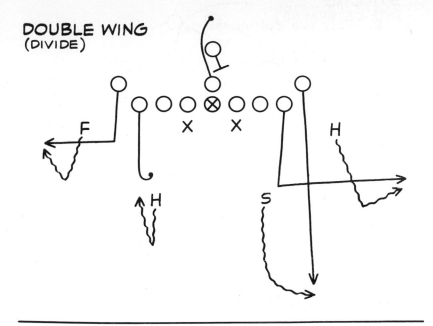

DOUBLE WING
(MOTION)

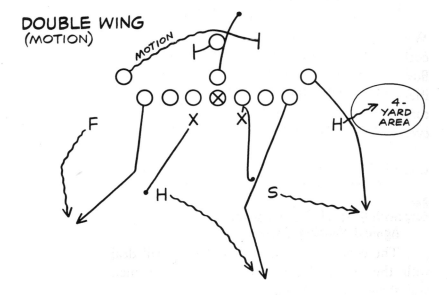

NOTE: WHAT IS IT WHEN THE BALL IS SNAPPED?

Figure 25

The safetyman calls, "box-set" when one of the following situations exists:

1. When one end spreads eight yards or more.

2. When two opposite ends spread eight yards or more.

3. When the opponent spreads an end eight yards, or more, to one side of the formation and simultaneously flanks a back eight yards to the opposite side.

4. When our Victory defense (used late in each half) has been called or when we are playing a 54 or 61 defensive alignment inside our own 10-yard line. At this time—if we are using box coverage—we want to be in box-set, playing man-for-man responsibilities within a zone.

5. When opponent comes out in a wildly outlandish formation that is unconventional and is used primarily to upset the defense. Under these circumstances, we line up in box-set across the field.

When box-set coverage is used, we do not rotate, cock, pre-determine or flow. In fact, we ignore flow, line up across the field, watch our responsibilities, play the ball once it is passed, and follow the cardinal rule of pass defense: no one gets behind us, ever.

Figure 26 shows a typical formation that we would use box-set coverage against.

Responsibilities of Four-Deep Men Against Running Game

The concluding part of this chapter will deal with the responsibilities of the four-deep men against the running game.

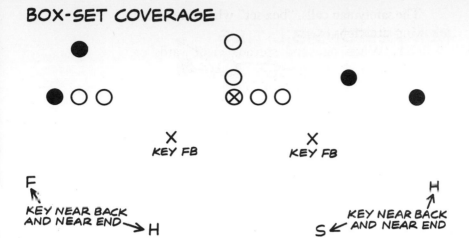

BOX-SET COVERAGE

Figure 26

Figure 27 shows the correct routes of approach our four-deep backs are taught to use when meeting a running play *(see page 160).*

When the play goes the opposite direction, their duties would be repeated. Once the play has been established as a definite run (using the keys discussed in Chapter Five), the corner linebackers and safetymen have the following responsibilities.

Corner linebackers. *When attacked by a running play . . .*

When the corner linebackers are attacked by a definitely established running play, they move up to the line of scrimmage using the same techniques as when they are attacked by flow on a pass (described earlier in this chapter under pass defense responsibilities).

RUN RESPONSIBILITIES

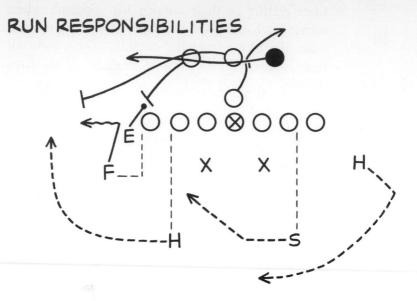

Figure 27

Their job is to force the play on the line of scrimmage. They do not commit into the opponent's backfield or open a large gap to their inside (the most frequent mistake a corner linebacker make) to give the offense room to maneuver.

They must know what their end is doing and maintain a constant two-yard area between themselves and the end man on the line of scrimmage. Their primary function is to delay the play until help comes from internal pursuit and rotating backs. The safety, to their inside, rotates to the outside to give help in that area.

Corner linebackers can solve their problems by using the following rules of conduct. First, when playing a blocker, they keep their feet parallel to the line of scrimmage so as to prevent the blocker

Four-Deep Pass Defense Coverage

from getting at their outside leg. Second, when corner linebackers are attacked, they move up and make the tackle from the outside. They make all their tackles with their inside shoulder. This stops the play.

When the running play goes away . . .

When the running play goes away from the corner linebacker, he follows the same procedure as when flow goes away on a pass. (This maneuver was described earlier in the chapter under the heading Pass Coverage Responsibilities.) It is important to stress with the corner linebackers, when the running play goes away from them, that they rotate to a three-deep halfback position *after* they move away from the line of scrimmage at a 45 degree angle. From the halfback position they play for the cutback and long run. They should not, in normal conditions, be making tackles across the field. They always leave the halfback position cautiously.

Safetyman. *When his near corner linebacker is attacked by a run . . .*

When the corner linebacker, next to either of the safetymen, is attacked by a definite running play the safetyman rotates up and to the outside of the corner linebacker, next to him.

As the safetyman rotates he keeps leverage on every offensive man. He supports his near corner linebacker from the *outside*—keeping his head on the outside shoulder of the widest man coming at him out of the opponent's backfield. The safetyman's responsibility is to turn the play in, get help from the internal pursuit and rotating backs, then make the tackle from the outside.

The rotated halfback must be aggressive but remain under control. His rule: NUMBER ONE IS THE PASS, NUMBER TWO IS THE RUN.

When the running play goes away . . .

When the definitely established running play is going away from either of the safetymen, they move to a position where a three-deep safetyman plays. From this point he operates like the safety-man in three-deep coverage. He moves laterally in the direction of the running play, moving fast as the ball *but a step behind*. He must never overrun the ball. When the ball carrier turns upfield the safety-man goes straight at the ball carrier. He is responsible for cut-backs from the off-tackle hole.

If the ball carrier continues on a wide end run, the safetyman keeps moving laterally with him, running as fast but a step behind.

The safetyman must be a "no-mistakes" man. He is the last line of defense. If he is caught in the open field against a ball carrier—with or without blockers—he fights a delaying action by dodging, feinting, hand-fighting and using the sidelines to help him. The safetyman does not commit quickly but rather is careful and makes sure. He keeps his poise and remembers that his job is to prevent touchdowns—not first downs.

Four-Deep Pass Defense Coverage

Teaching

Pass Defense

in Early Season Practice

Chapter Seven

BEFORE discussing our theories and methods of teaching pass defense in early season practice—I must reiterate the emphasis that we put on being mentally prepared to play pass defense in addition to the learning and execution of principles, responsibilities, and techniques.

Pass defense, to me, is largely a matter of desiring to excel, so we continually stress the importance of having the proper frame of mind. The pass defender must want to play pass defense and be mentally ready. The right mental approach, when playing football, is as important as possessing the necessary physical attributes; often more so.

A large amount of practice is necessary to the development of good pass defense, beginning with the opening day of spring and/or early season practice right through to the last day of the season. During early season practice 30 to 40 minutes is allotted to pass defense in each two-hour practice, and 90 percent of all pass defense work (the first four days) is devoted to drills. Devoting substantial amounts of time *daily* is necessary because of the many varied techniques, principles, and responsibilities the pass defender must learn, execute and perfect to become an accomplished pass defense man.

After the individuals have mastered the techniques necessary to play good pass defense, they must be molded into a cohesive unit before an effective pass defense can be realized.

A good pass defense is built in early season practice. Like a house, pass defense must be built on a good foundation, so utmost care must be given to the building of that foundation; everything that follows will be dependent upon a solid foundation of fundamentals, principles, belief and execution.

We always teach pass defense on a lined football field. This gives the defenders perspective regarding their field positions, which is very important to learning good pass defense. Players must always know where they are in relation to the sidelines and goal line. A team that practices pass defense on an unmarked field is wasting valuable time.

Simplicity must be stressed and maintained during this important phase of teaching pass defense (the first days of spring or early season practice). All learning must take place in progression. Players must learn steps one and two before three is taught. Avoid any duplication of terminology. For instance, a back is *always* a flanked back, an end is *always* a spread end, never vice-versa.

Basic principles and responsibilities taught during early season practice must be lucid and remain constant. The coach uses a positive approach in all his teaching methods—there can be no fluctuating. When teaching a specific point the coach cannot allow himself to say "if this happens, *etcetera.*" He must say "*when* this happens, you do this, *etcetera.*" The negative approach of teaching causes doubt, and hesitation will then lead to a breakdown of the pass defense.

Pass defenders must learn *by doing.* I believe in the 10 to 1 ratio when teaching pass defense: Tell players once and have them execute ten times!

Maintaining verbal communication between defenders is stressed from the outset of practice. By talking to each other, the pass defense men gain

Teaching Pass Defense in Early Season Practice

cohesion, avoid confusion and reduce mistakes. The importance of talking to each other was amplified in Chapter Four under basic principles of pass defense. It is repeated here because of its importance.

We do not believe in over-coaching the individual in pass defense—particularly the good ones. The challenge facing the coach, when teaching adept pass defenders, is to harness and channel their aptitudes so they are executing correctly and getting maximum performance from their innate abilities.

The real test of a coach is to build a boy who is not endowed with any appreciable aptitude for pass defense into a strong pass defense man. This is the *real* satisfaction in coaching—to build a weak spot into a strong point.

During this crucial stage in the development of a good pass defense, we continually remind the defensive personnel of the strengths and weaknesses of each defensive game and pass coverage being used. We have found, through experience, that this also will help develop a feeling for what we are doing on pass defense.

Individual Work

We have three objectives in individual work:

1. To build a solid foundation for the pass defense

2. To teach the basic principles of pass defense.

3. To determine the pass defense capabilities of each player

To achieve these objectives we do the following things.

Use a Large Number of Drills

The first thing that is done in individual work during early season practice is to teach and execute drills. Drills are important in teaching any phase of football, but particularly pass defense. We use many drills and spend a large amount of time on them. Drills to be effective must be run at least four times in every practice session and possibly more—depending on individual differences and the game maturity of the participating players. Drills must simulate game conditions, have meaning for the players, and should "teach by doing." (Chapter Nine is devoted to the discussion of pass defense drills.)

Establish a Classroom on the Field

When any phase of pass defense is taught for the first time on the field, we explain it very carefully. After that the question-and-answer method of learning is used. The players are asked questions and they answer them—then we know that *they* know. What we actually do is establish a classroom on the field.

All facets of pass defense are learned using this teaching technique. It has been a revelation to see how much can be learned and *retained* by the players in a short period of time.

Run Individual Pass Patterns Against Individual Defenders

Once the pass defense men know their principles, responsibilities and techniques, we run patterns against them.

It is particularly necessary at this stage of the pass defense's development to keep pass patterns simple. The coach must control the patterns that the offensive men are running. Beginning with the fundamental pass routes, the coach directs the receiver to run patterns ever more difficult to cover.

Eventually the pass defender must cover—on an individual basis—all of the basic pass "cuts." Each man must be brought along at his own particular speed. Pass patterns that the defender must cover include the hook, square-out, square-in, deep, deep and flag, deep and across, and the question mark pass.

Pitting one defender against one offensive receiver will very quickly reveal the strengths and weaknesses of each defender against each of the basic pass patterns. The coach then knows which pass pattern gives a particular defender trouble. As a result the coach can help the player—in an intelligent and positive manner—by running repeatedly the pass "cut" against which the defender is weakest. It is not necessary to repeatedly run the pattern that a defender successfully covers, but it is important to work against the pass that the defender has trouble covering.

Now Add Two-Man Pass Patterns

When the individual pass defender has mastered the techniques of covering the basic patterns, the next step in our progressive learning is to have two pass defenders cover two men running pass routes.

Again, as when the pass defenders were first exposed to individual patterns, it is imperative that only simple patterns be run at first. Pass routes such as double hooks, double deeps, double square-outs, and double square-ins should be used.

The coach at this time forbids any crossing or "change-for-depth" patterns. The coach must allow the pass defense to have success. Running difficult patterns which they cannot cover will wreck the confidence of individual defenders before they have "gotten their feet on the ground." This is bad coaching for it will take considerable time and work to restore the confidence that was lost.

Again—it is utterly important to control this phase of learning in the construction of the pass defense.

The next step, after confidence in coverage of double patterns has been gained, is to introduce *simple crossing patterns*. Begin by making receivers run slowly through crossing pass routes and allow the pass defender to enjoy success. Pass defense men must execute their correct fundamentals, principles and responsibilities, but also make the passer throw an arc-type pass that will encourage Jerichoes.

At this state of development the men playing pass defense must concentrate on:

1. Proper coverage
2. Jerichoes
3. Knocking the ball down

When the pass defense, as a unit, has reached this stage of maturity the coach must make sure that the individual men are gaining understanding. They can go through the individual techniques perfectly and still not be getting a picture of the *over-all* pass defense.

They should now be getting a grasp of the total

Teaching Pass Defense in Early Season Practice

concept of pass defense. In this highly specialized phase of football, improvement in a team's pass defense is in direct proportion to the individual's improvement, both as a single defender and a responsive part of a well-knit unit.

Group Work

Once we reach the group work stage of teaching pass defense, the coach begins to put the parts together.

When group work begins, we put colored half shirts on those backs who are our keys and the pass defense coach works as the quarterback, directly behind the demonstrating offensive team. By doing this he can control formations, pass patterns, their frequency and also can specify the personnel that will run against the pass defenders. Also, he can watch the defenders' eyes, look for star-gazers, and their resulting reactions and coverage. It is very easy from this vantage point to anticipate and correct mistakes as they are readily discernible.

The pass defense is now moving into its second stage of development and it is more important than ever to run simple patterns and to allow the defenders some success. At this stage of development, we never destroy the pass defense morale and confidence with unorthodox patterns and odd formations.

The passer is allowed only 3.5 seconds to throw the ball, to simulate game-like conditions. This is all the time he will get to throw in a game. Therefore, he should not be allowed any more time to throw in practice. There are no defensive linemen available to put "pressure" on him in pass defense practice, so we must use a time limit. The passer should not be allowed to have "all day" to pass and, as a result, riddle the pass defense. Any passer can complete passes if he has enough time to throw the ball. At no time in our pass defense practice is a demonstrating passer allowed more than 3.5 seconds to deliver the ball.

As the pass defense develops we review principles constantly and also maintain the question-and-answer method of teaching. The pass patterns steadily get tougher and more complicated but only as the pass defender's belief gets stronger, his confidence grows, and his understanding becomes more evident. Also, it is imperative that the men who defend against the pass keep talking to each other during all phases of learning.

When they have mastered principles, techniques and responsibilities, the defenders must now react and be allowed to make mistakes. They can learn from their mistakes. They have reached a certain maturity now, so mistakes will not bother them or destroy their morale, as it might the young, inexperienced defender. Mistakes will spur the experienced defender to work on his weaknesses and develop him into a better pass defense man.

Now it is time to run more difficult patterns against the pass defense and test defenders under fire.

The next step in pass defense maturity is to show them—on the field—all the formations they will probably play against during the coming football season.

The defenders go through their adjustments and responsibilities against each formation shown to them.

All the while, we ask questions of the boys involved in pass defense on all facets of pass defense coverage. This way we know that *they* know.

Practicing

Pass Defense

During the Season

Chapter Eight

PASS defense practice, once early season drills are completed, changes perceptibly. Pass defense practice has a different emphasis during the season. Our objective now is to "jell" the pass defense into a cohesive unit while still working with individuals Now we are also drilling against specific pass patterns of the next opponent.

During the early season practice, the individual is given a great deal of attention. Fundamentals regarding principles, responsibilities and techniques are stressed. We are looking for the parts with which to assemble the whole complete unit. Once the season begins, emphasis is on what the unit can stop, their strengths and weaknesses, and we work from there.

When a boy displays the necessary ability to play pass defense, the coach then must develop that boy's abilities to the point where he will carry his share of the load in defending against enemy aerials. He will grow stronger by just being a part of a unit; his strengths may be a fellow defender's weakness and vice versa. As a result of playing together, each will get stronger as pass defense men. The feeling we want to build in our pass defense men—once the teaching, drill work and experimental stage of early season practice is finished—is this: we now are a unit and must develop into a cohesive, flexible, "gung-ho" group which wants the opponent to throw the ball against us because the ball will then be ours.

Learn the Opponent's Pass Tendencies

Much time is spent analyzing scouts' reports and movie breakdowns to find an opponent's passing tendencies. We then carefully instruct our pass defense men to take advantage of any tendencies that are apparent.

Teaching them to capitalize on any tendencies is accomplished *on the field* throughout the week. (I am not a "blackboard coach.") Anything that is to be meaningful to the pass defense *must* be taught on the football field. Tendencies are taught by moving the pass defense to different field positions—using both hash marks and the middle of the field—then the tactical situation is announced. Pass defense men react to the call by identifying the pass they expect.

Playing situations and tendencies is fine when they are definitely established, but discretion must be exercised in dealing with this phase of football. A team can get burned badly by believing and following tendencies and situations too religiously. They should be used as more of an indication rather than as an infallible truth.

Here is another wrinkle that has helped our pass defense. During the season—when working against the opponent's passes—our *defensive* backs run the pass patterns from the offensive position which they will be responsible for during the next game. Running the pass routes that they will defend against on Saturday gives our defenders knowledge, understanding and appreciation of the patterns and of the men they will be covering during the game.

Practicing Pass Defense During the Season

Assemble, Analyze and Chart
Opponent's Passes

In the process of preparing to defend against a specific opponent's passes, we first assemble all their passes. They are secured from scouts' reports, in-season movie exchange, and the movie breakdown from the previous year's game. Also included are any passes that hurt us in previous games. We will see those again for sure!

Once all the enemy passes are assembled and analyzed, we then discard any that are used only a negligible number of times, or that should be covered well without working against them.

After this is accomplished, the passes are charted—by usage, formation and effectiveness—on 12 x 15 white cards (four passes to a card, front and back). Notes are made on the cards with pertinent information concerning touchdown passes, the tactical and field situation from which *choice* passes are thrown. Also, a particular pass which the opponent used successfully against us in the past is noted.

Using this procedure, it has been necessary to carry but two or three cards on the field. They contain all the information that is needed.

There are three things that must be done in every pass defense practice, *every* day of the week, throughout the football season.

1. Every player involved in pass defense must practice his footwork drill before organized practice starts.
2. The pass defenders must maintain verbal communication with each other at all times.

3. The demonstrating passer is allowed only 3.5 seconds to throw the football.

Practice Organization

Before discussing our pass defense practice plans it is necessary to explain our over-all team practice organization. Our staff is divided into offensive and defensive coaches. We run simultaneous practices with two units working on separate fields. Both units learn offense and defense. We prepare two and one-half boys, at each position, to play in the game.

Following is the practice plan our pass defense follows each week during the football season:

MONDAY

(10 minutes per group—no pads)

The players are in sweat clothes, but they wear their helmets. (Our players always wear their football helmets on the field—with or without pads.)

We carefully explain the opponent's formations, their personnel (receivers and passers), their big passes and their over-all offensive philosophy, (ratio of passes to runs).

Next, the pass defenders are lined up (in special then box coverage) against the opponent's formations. Their keys and responsibilities are reviewed and at this time any changes deemed necessary in preparing for the next opponent are made. Any changes or exceptions to our principles are kept to a minimum.

Practicing Pass Defense During the Season

The pass defense on Monday will see only the opponent's three or four best passes. These are the passes we must stop to render the adversary's passing attack ineffective.

Monday's practice is devoted to preparing the pass defenders mentally for the type of passer and passing attack they will play against on Saturday.

TUESDAY

(20 minutes per group—in pads)

Once the season begins, we spend very little time in organized practice drills.

On Tuesday, all the passes are thrown that the pass defense will probably see in the next game—but none they will not see.

Practice time is divided according to the proportion of three-deep (special) and four-deep (box) coverage that we plan to use in the game. This is dependent on our defensive game plan for the next opponent.

When possible we work unit A against unit B on pass defense. If this cannot be done, then we secure the fastest boys available to run pass patterns against the pass defense. We want the pass defense to see the best, because they cannot speed up on Saturday. I am a firm believer in the old football adage: "As you practice, so you play."

The pass defense coach continues to work behind the demonstrating team. I am *never* behind the pass defense on the practice field—for reasons stated in Chapter Seven. In addition to the reasons already cited, we can (by working from this vantage point), repeat a pass pattern without asking for it.

Also, I can see if the demonstrating ends and backs are running the opponent's patterns correctly.

It is also easy to check a specific pass defender against a particular pass quickly and without his knowing it. I am completely sold on working behind the demonstrating team when coaching the pass defense.

Tuesday is a learning day, but we stress verbally that certain passes can and must be covered by the pass defense without practicing against them specifically. We are not content with ordinary performance on Tuesday. We want complete coverage and no mental sloppiness regarding responsibilities is accepted. On Tuesday the pass defenders are pushed, needled, and if need be, irritated—if the situation demands it. They must be rough and aggressive. This is the night to set the tempo for Saturday.

Later in practice, during team defense, the demonstrating team throws passes once in every five plays that are run against the defensive team. This keeps the secondary alert and also gives them game situation perspective.

WEDNESDAY

(15 minutes per group—in pads)

We continue to work against the opponent's passes by formation, frequency, effectiveness and situation, but now the number of *different* passes thrown against the pass defense is cut down. There is no need, on Wednesday, for the pass defense to see passes that the opposition has used but once or twice. The exception would be a favorite or scoring pass.

By now the pass defense should understand the opponent's over-all pass offense. Also, they must be aware of this ever-present pass defense truth. Regardless of how many passes are scouted, charted and worked against, somewhere in a game the pass defense must cover a pass they have never seen or drilled against in practice. The pass defense—if it is to be worth its name must be able to cope with such situations when they arise.

Periodically during Wednesday practice the draw play is run to keep the pass defense honest and thinking. This is the practice where good coverage should be apparent. The pass defense by now must have insight into the next opponent's passing attack.

We continue to pass once in every five plays run against the varsity in team defense drills.

At the conclusion of team practice on Wednesday the backs get their tackling practice, against the two-man sleds. Once the season begins we do not scrimmage the backs during the week. Seldom, if ever, do they have live tackling practice. I cannot remember the last time it was done at Rutgers.

Tackling is 90 percent desire and 10 percent technique. The correct technique is drilled into the backs while they are tackling the two-man sleds. Each back tackles the sled three times, emphasizing correct approach, proper body position, good contact and follow-through. This is the extent of in-season tackling practice for the backs. We do not want a riproaring head-on tackling drill Wednesday that will leave any of our better backs injured so they cannot play Saturday. This would nullify all we are attempting to accomplish. They must be ready to play a good football game on Saturday.

THURSDAY

(15 minutes per group—no pads)

In Thursday practice, the number of different passes thrown against the pass defense is cut to a minimum. We are now concentrating on the opponent's four or five best passes.

The pass defense should be executing well by Thursday against all passes. They should not be extra sharp (their peak must be reached on Saturday), but they should know and understand what they are covering.

We do not "kill" the pass defense now. If something is wrong, we remedy it rather than continue to get poor coverage. This is Thursday and the game is only two days away. What the pass defense does in this practice session will directly reflect in their performance on Saturday.

It is very important to close Thursday pass defense practice on a positive note. Leave the boys with the conviction that they will cover all passes the enemy will throw at them in the game—and Jericho one in every eight!

FRIDAY

Friday is a warm-up day with no pass defense practice. There should be no coaching done on Friday. Do not ever—under any circumstances—change coverage, make radical changes, or start to

Practicing Pass Defense During the Season

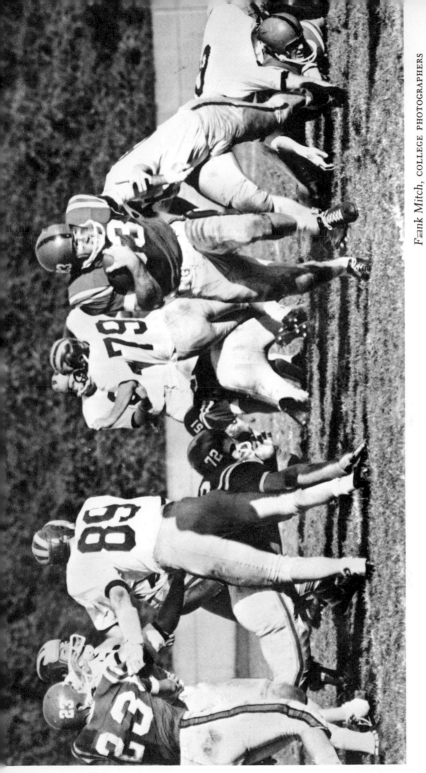

F=nk Mitch, COLLEGE PHOTOGRAPHERS

Figure 27a: Steve Simms, **Rutgers'** 1961 All- Eastern fullback, demonstrates his powerful running technique against **Delaware.**

second-guess yourself concerning a particular pass that may have "hurt" the defense during the week. This negative thinking will very quickly permeate the squad and they will begin to absorb your doubts. If this is allowed to happen, the pass defense will be ineffective Saturday.

Friday is no time for negative thoughts. We want our defenders to leave the practice field feeling that every time the enemy throws the football in tomorrow's game it is being thrown to us.

Drills

in Pass Defense

Chapter Nine

GOOD drills are necessary to the development of a sound pass defense. One of the best ways to improve an athlete's ability and make him an outstanding pass defense man is to have him do over and over the things he must do during a game. This is accomplished only through drills.

A drill to be effective must simulate game conditions and situations, which means wearing helmets during all drills. It must have meaning to the player and he must know what the drill is meant to accomplish. There must be "player-insight" regarding the drill: why is it being done?

Drills should teach the basic fundamentals for a successful pass defense. When a player performs the fundamentals well, he is usually a good pass defender. The exception to this statement of course is a boy who does not possess the quality "X"—the ability to produce in a game situation.

Good drills teach specific techniques, develop reactions, and aid in conditioning all at once. They should be varied, interesting, carefully planned, and organized, so the players will both learn from the drills and enjoy executing them.

When working on drills, strict attention must be given to little things, stressing the teaching of fundamentals and the correction of individual faults. Through drills the coach can work on ways to improve the individual pass defender. We believe that drills are the most important factor in improving a pass defender.

Regardless of the quality or quantity of drills

used or the techniques taught, nothing will succeed in producing a good pass defense *unless* the players have the proper mental attitude. The secondary pass defense men must have an insatiable desire to play pass defense and take justifiable pride in their accomplishments. Good drills can help instill this pride and desire.

This chapter contains a number of pass defense drills that have been helpful and effective for us.

Footwork Drill

This drill is used to develop both techniques and good reaction. It is not primarily a conditioning drill. A good pass defender must master the art of running away from the line of scrimmage, with the upper body and head looking through the potential receiver to the passer. (i.e., from the waist *down* the defender runs toward one goal line—from the waist *up* he faces the opposite goal line.)

The footwork drill helps a player master the all-important aforementioned technique that is paramount in the development of a good pass defender. This drill embodies all the basic skills a boy must learn and execute to become a good pass defender. For this reason it is our number one drill.

We have found that freshmen are, inevitably, clumsy when they begin the footwork drill, but with constant work and repetition they become very proficient and develop into outstanding pass defenders as a result of working on all facets of this drill.

Our varsity pass defense men are told on the first day of practice that they can cover any end or

Drills in Pass Defense

back they will play against during their collegiate career by using the footwork maneuver correctly.

The drill can be performed alone, in pairs, or groups, and can be used with or without a football.

Footwork drill alone. We begin teaching the footwork drill by placing a pass defender directly in front of and facing the coach at a distance of five yards. All other players in the drill line up in single file line to the right of the coach. (See *Figure 28*.) The player on defense assumes his proper position; safetymen and inside linebackers use the parallel stance; halfbacks and corner linebackers use the staggered stance with the outside leg free.

On the command, "go," the pass defender begins to run backward. His first step is back at an angle, using the open then the cross-over step (left over right). On the second command, "cut," the defender plants his back foot, lowers his body, pivots on the planted foot, rolls his hips, and changes direction from right to left or vice versa. We do not want the pass defender to back-pedal. Going to the footwork maneuver immediately and not using the back-pedal or boxer's shuffle step has helped us greatly in preventing long pass completions, either for long yardage or touchdowns.

When pass defense men are doing the footwork drill alone they must always keep their vision on the imaginary receiver while looking through to the passer. The defender works on a straight line—not in a zig-zag course.

After the defender has mastered this maneuver, the coach throws the football to the pass defender, with varying degrees of difficulty, as he is running backward. The purpose of this is to make the pass

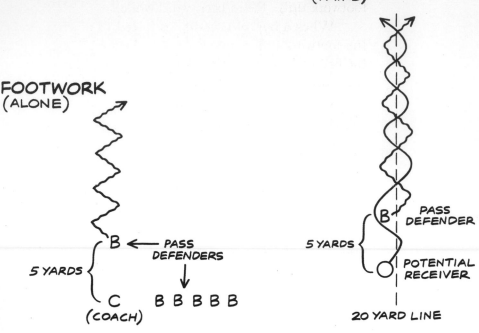

FOOTWORK
(ALONE)

5 YARDS { B ← PASS DEFENDERS

C   B B B B B
(COACH)

FOOTWORK
(PAIRS)

5 YARDS { B PASS DEFENDER

POTENTIAL RECEIVER

20 YARD LINE

Figure 28   **Figure 29**

defender react to the pass while running away from the ball. He must come up with the ball.

Another innovation we have added, when using the footwork drill alone, is to start the pass defender going backward. Then on the command, "*return*," he plants his back foot and sprints back to the coach. We find that on the command, "*return*," most players when stopping will either skip, take an extra step, or slip and fall down. This is where many pass defenders are beaten in ball

Drills in Pass Defense

games, so we work frequently on this phase of the footwork drill. It has been worthwhile.

When a boy, of necessity, is forced to practice the footwork drill without a coach, he simply uses the first phase of the drill as has been described here and calls his own "cut" signal.

Footwork drill in pairs. This is the next step in the development of the footwork drill. Each defender pairs up with another defender on the yard lines going across the football field. (See Figure 9.) One player is on offense and the other on defense. They take turns taking each other across the field, using the footwork maneuver, and returning. Going over, one boy will be the potential receiver—the other will be the pass defender. Returning, the procedure is reversed.

The defensive man assumes his correct position five yards away from the receiver. The offensive man runs at half-speed, cutting back and forth at 45 degree angles all the while the defender is maintaining a straight course across the field. Later, when the defender has mastered the footwork maneuver, the offensive man runs at full speed.

During this phase of the drill several important points are stressed. First, the defender must always keep the pass receiver in line of vision with the passer. He must always maintain leverage on the potential receiver and look through him to the passer. The defender focuses his eyes on the pass receiver's belt buckle—where it goes he goes too! Secondly, he never allows the pass receiver to get within four yards of him—if so, he's licked. No one gets behind the defender, ever. This part of the footwork drill is practiced by all pass defense men every day of the season from opening day of pre-season drills to the last day of practice.

The next development of this drill, when defenders are paired off against each other, is throwing the ball to the defender as he is moving backward and away from the passer. The pass defender must learn to catch the football as he is running backwards and away from the ball. This is quite different from catching the ball on offense or moving into the ball on defense.

When we throw the ball in this drill this point is stressed with the pass defenders: until the football is thrown, the pass defender gives the potential receiver 100 percent of his attention. Once the ball is passed the defender gives 100 percent of his attention to *the ball*.

After the ball is thrown, the defender leaves man and "flies to the ball." It is the only ball in the game so he must give it his undivided attention.

When going for the ball, the defender must stretch his arms and hands to the maximum, play through the man, look the ball into his hands, catch the ball at its highest point, then put it away and run for a touchdown. With each succeeding pass, we seek to increase the distance the defender can go to get the football.

We also drill on footwork by having the pass defense man sprint for 30 yards using only the footwork maneuver. All players involved in pass defense are lined up on the 30-yard line. On the coach's command they sprint to the goal line. This facet of the drill can be executed either alone or with an offensive pass receiver.

It is done best with a potential receiver running alongside so the defender can practice all his pass defense fundamentals as outlined previously. During this drill we tell the defenders that if the offensive man makes his cut while running at full speed, the pass defenders must plant their back foot, pivot, and roll their hips. This will automatically keep them in the proper position with good leverage on the potential receiver.

In group footwork drill (Figure 30), pass defenders line up across the field on the 30-yard line five yards apart. Another row is lined up on the 20-yard line directly behind the first. Make as many rows as necessary to include all pass defense men.

The coach faces the group with a football in

FOOTWORK
(GROUP)

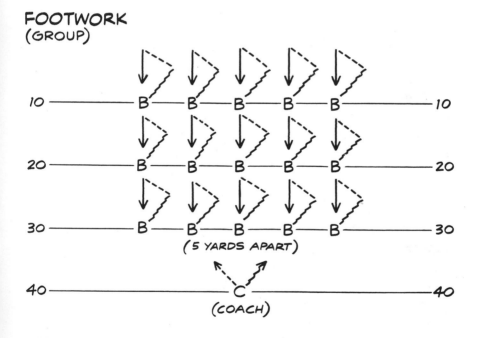

Figure 30

his hands. He uses the ball to give directions. When the ball is pointed to the right the defenders break in that direction, using proper footwork; when the coach points to the left they move in that direction. Holding the ball against his stomach is the coach's signal for the defenders to run backward at full speed—using the footwork steps. To bring the defenders forward the coach cocks the ball behind his ear.

The final part of this group footwork drill is to throw the ball to a specific defender while the pass defenders are executing any one of the four aforementioned maneuvers. Every pass defender in the drill must "fly to the ball" with the purpose of getting a Jericho.

Another drill we use in teaching good footwork technique is as follows:

Group footwork drill. We work in groups of three men spaced five yards apart (*Figure 31*). The coach stands in front and gives the command, "ready—set," and the pass defenders assume their correct defensive stance.

The coach lifts a football to passing position. The players will react to this maneuver by driving straight back with their knees bent, hips lowered, and arms hanging loose. The footwork maneuver is used while the defenders do this. As they move back at an angle they must watch the coach, who moves the ball from left to right across his chest. The defenders react to the indicated direction, rolling their hips, "watching the belt buckle," and maintaining vision.

When the coach brings the ball down, the defenders drive forward. The ball is occasionally thrown to them. They must be alert. In this drill we let them go at least five yards but never more than 10. The distance is varied so they cannot anticipate and pace themselves; they *must* react to the ball.

Tipping Drill

This is a reaction drill. It not only teaches pass defenders quickness and agility in reacting to a deflected ball, but also gives them added incentive to get the football when it is thrown.

Line up all the defensive backs in single file facing the coach (or a passer) who is 20 yards away. (See *Figure* 32.) Alongside the first back in the line place a large blocking dummy, which impersonates the potential receiver.

On a signal from the coach the first man in

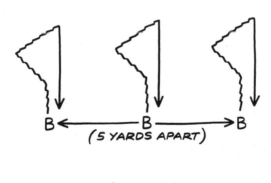

B ← ———— B ———— → B
(5 YARDS APART)

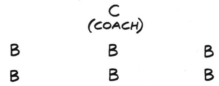

C
(COACH)

B   B   B

B   B   B

Figure 31

line runs toward the coach. When he gets five yards away from his original position the second man starts to run also directly behind the first man toward the coach.

The coach throws the ball at the first man who tips the ball backward, using a volleyball tap. The second player catches the ball, calls out *Jericho*, puts the ball away, sprints to the coach, and *hands* him the ball. Doing this eliminates chasing the ball, broken noses, sprained fingers, etc.

After the first player tips the ball he whirls around and knocks down the dummy impersonating the potential receiver. We want to eliminate him, *always*, on every Jericho.

TIPPING

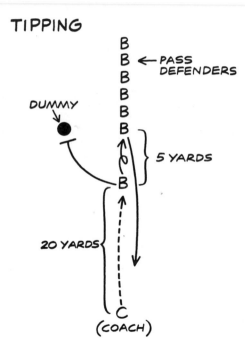

Figure 32

Drills in Pass Defense

The coach should throw the ball at the head or shoulders of the first man. Stress the importance of the defensive back reacting quickly to the loose ball. The second man *must* catch the ball no matter what its position or height. He must *be alert*. A coaching point: Do not allow the two men to break until the coach has the ball in his hands.

We have a variation that is used in the tipping drill. The first man *may* or *may not* tip the ball. The second man must react and catch the ball in either situation. We have found that many Jerichoes are made by defenders leaving their man and going for the ball but only when it is thrown. It takes a good defender to cover one-on-one and get a Jericho. However, if he can achieve good position, many times the ball will be deflected and one of his fellow pass defenders coming to help will make the Jericho.

Another variation of the tipping drill is shown in *Figure 33*.

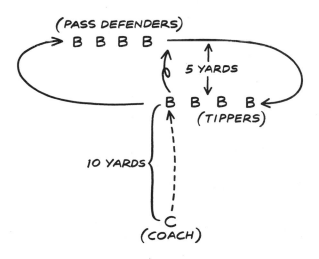

Figure 33

Drills in Pass Defense

Line up six "tippers" in single file on the 10-yard line, stretching across the field and facing the opposite sideline. This line occupies an area from mid-field to the right sideline. Another line of tippers—the exact opposite of the one described—is placed on the 15-yard line. This line, facing mid-field, stretches from the left sideline to the middle of the field. The first man in each line runs toward the center of the field. From 10 yards distance, the coach throws the ball straight down the middle of the field. The "tipper" in the first line tips the ball and the player in the second line reacts to it. From then on, the drill follows the same procedure as the original tipping drill. This introduces the factor of lateral motion, a typical game situation.

Slap the Ball Drill

The purpose of this drill is to teach the pass defender to slap the ball to the ground when he can not intercept, thereby preventing any opportunity for the offense to catch a pass that a defender meant to knock down. Many passes are completed and games are won or lost when a lazy pass defender does not "bang" the ball to the ground but flicks it into the air where an alert waiting receiver catches it for a completed pass and possible touchdown.

The slap drill (Figure 34) is executed in the same way as the tipping drill, but only one player runs toward the coach on signal. The coach throws the ball hard or soft, high or low, directly at the defender or away. Regardless of where the ball is thrown, the important point is that the defender *slaps* the ball to the ground if he can not get the Jericho. This drill is very simple but has proved to be worthwhile.

Drills in Pass Defense

SLAP THE BALL

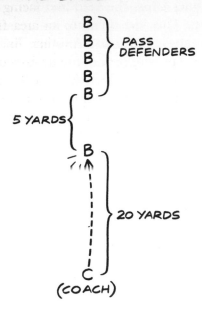

Figure 34

Bad Pass Drill

The pass defenders form in single file facing the coach who is 10 yards away (see *Figure 35*). On the signal from the coach the first man will run toward him. The player does not "break" until the coach has the football in his hands. Beginning at half-speed and working up to full speed, the defenders, one at a time and as fast as the coach can throw the ball, will run toward him. As they run the coach will throw the football at various spots, starting with the high, hard pass to make the pass defender stretch his arms and *catch the ball at its highest point.* At other times it will be at shoe top level. Make the pass defender work. He must move toward the ball and learn to hold on to it—regardless of the speed or position of the ball or body. When the ball is caught the defender calls out, "*Jericho.*"

The point to stress in this drill is that in a game, when making a Jericho the pass defender most of the time will be running or moving *toward the passer or ball.* There is a great difference between catching the ball as a pass receiver on offense and catching it as a pass defender on defense. As in other drills, the players hand the ball to the coach as they run by him. This prevents wasting time chasing badly thrown footballs.

A second step in this drill is to make two parallel lines five yards apart facing the same direction and lining up the same distance (10 yards)

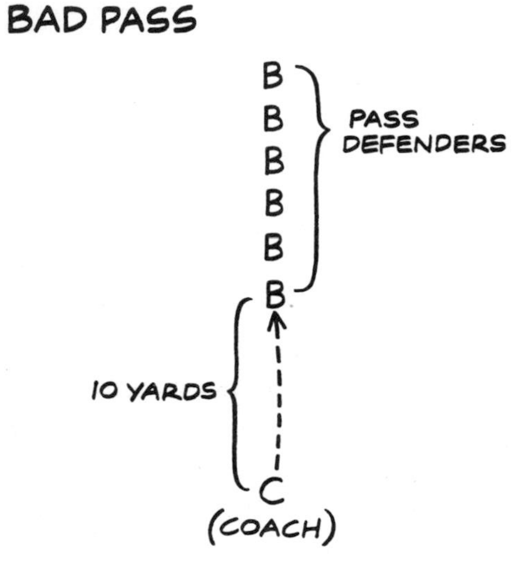

BAD PASS

Figure 35

Drills in Pass Defense

away (see *Figure 36*). On the coach's signal, the first two backs in each line break toward the coach. He throws the ball down the middle between the two breaking pass defenders.

Two things are emphasized in this drill: First, one of the two defenders must get the football for a Jericho; second, the defender, if a Jericho is impossible, knocks the ball down. Good defenders must not give up the ball easily. This is important, for *in a simultaneous catch, the offense gets the football.*

Pass defenders must time their jump to meet the ball at the highest point. They should ignore physical contact with the opponent and fight *only* for the ball. For competition in this drill we pit the left halfbacks against the right halfbacks, quarterbacks against fullbacks.

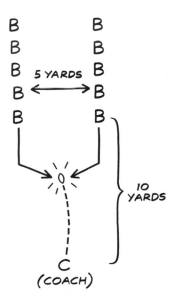

Figure 36

Drills in Pass Defense

Another innovation we have added in this drill is to do the same thing as just described but have the pass defenders going away from the coach rather than toward him.

Jericho Drill

This drill is based on our belief that in 90 percent of all interceptions, the pass defender making the Jericho is tackled by the intended receiver, thus destroying any opportunity for a demoralizing long return.

The purpose of the Jericho drill is to eliminate the intended receiver—by knocking him down—once the Jericho is made.

Line up the pass defenders, including linebackers, in either the three- or four-deep secondary alignment. If a team uses both, call out clearly the specific alignment that is to be drilled at that particular time (see *Figure 37*).

Place three large blocking dummies (to simulate the intended receivers) at various spots in the secondary. The coach assumes the passer's position, with a complete backfield but no ends. All types of formations and pass offense techniques are used by the offense: the drop-back, roll-out, play-pass, and bootleg maneuvers. The coach checks for accurate adjustments, correct reaction to keys, eye-control, and swift reaction to the thrown ball.

The passer throws the ball to any one of the pass defenders. When we first start working on the Jericho drill the passer throws a high arching pass. This makes Jerichoes easier and serves to increase the defender's confidence in his ability both to cover the man he is responsible for and also to make the all-important Jericho.

Drills in Pass Defense

JERICHO DRILL

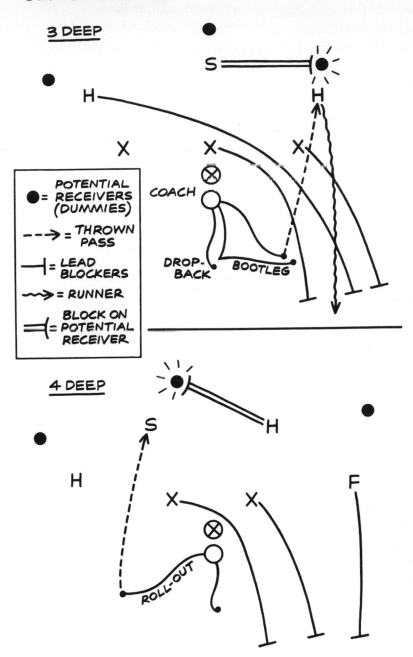

3 DEEP

POTENTIAL
● = RECEIVERS
(DUMMIES)

- - -> = THROWN PASS

+ = LEAD BLOCKERS

~~> = RUNNER

+ = BLOCK ON POTENTIAL RECEIVER

COACH

DROP-BACK   BOOTLEG

4 DEEP

ROLL-OUT

Figure 37

Once the ball is thrown and the pass defender catches it, he calls out, "Jericho." The call should be loud and clear!

This tells the defensive team that they are now on offense. It means, start throwing blocks! When "Jericho" is called out, the pass defender nearest to the interceptor knocks down the intended receiver. Make him actually throw the block on the dummy. Meanwhile all other pass defenders turn upfield as lead blockers. The defender making the Jericho is drilled to establish a threat up the middle, then head for the sideline. If he sees daylight, he can break this rule and run for the open area.

This drill has helped in getting longer returns on Jerichoes. In 1961 we returned Jerichoes for 405 yards, a 17.6 yard average per Jericho return. Needless to say, the Jericho drill is one of our most used drills.

Teach the men that once the ball is in the air, it is ours. Get it, then knock down the intended receiver.

Simultaneous Pass Defense —Pass Offense Drill

This drill provides opportunity to work on pass defense and pass offense simultaneously. The offense uses the complete pass offense with an occasional draw play. The defense works on pass defense.

The full football field is used along with a referee and scorer. Down and distance are factors. The offense is given the football on its own 20-yard line. Tactical situations, including time (the offense is allowed just four seconds to throw the ball) are played. The offense keeps the ball when the necessary yardage is made; otherwise the ball goes over to the defensive team.

The offense can use either seven men (tackles and guards out) or a complete team. The defense has the eight men involved in pass defense. The drill is competitive—offense versus defense. The ball can change hands at any time because the drill is conducted under game-like conditions and situations.

Following is the scoring used in the drill.

OFFENSE . . . 1 point for each yard gained by passing.

50 points for each touchdown pass.

DEFENSE . . . 2 points for an incomplete pass.

2 points when pass is not thrown in four seconds.

5 points for each pass knocked down.

25 points for a Jericho.

50 points for a Jericho returned for a touchdown.

The score is announced each time the ball changes hands. The drill runs for 20 minutes.

A word of warning for the pass defense regarding this drill. The simultaneous drill can be bewildering and frustrating to the defense if the pass offense uses flankers, spread ends, and motion before pass defense personnel have been taught the adjustments against these various formations. It is unwise to allow this to happen. Under these conditions the drill would be harmful and would not be accomplishing what it is meant to do.

Perception Drill

The purpose of this drill is to develop depth perception in the deep secondary pass defenders as they are moving forward toward the ball at full speed.

Station defensive halfbacks and a safetyman downfield 50 yards from the passer and facing him. The passer throws the ball 30 yards downfield as the halfbacks and safetyman are moving forward at full speed. The deep secondary men must judge the ball accurately and catch it at its highest point. To be effective this drill should be used often. (See Figure 38.)

One-Way Drill

In this drill the pass defenders are allowed to make only one move. We start two players off side by side two yards apart. (See Figure 39.) They go back on a signal from the coach (lifting the ball to a passing position). The defenders move back approximately 10 yards—the coach then points either left or right and they both make a square cut in the indicated direction. The coach throws the ball and both defenders go for it—either to Jericho the ball or to break it up by driving through the opponent. The coach varies his throw each time to pull one man wider or make one man come back. The defender who gets his hands on the ball must come up with it or knock it down.

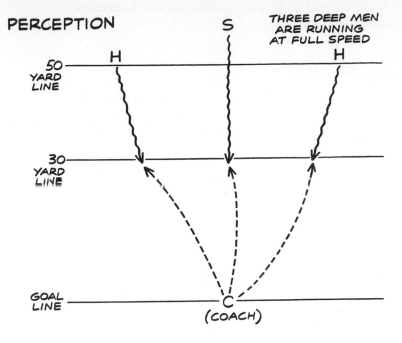

PERCEPTION

S

THREE DEEP MEN ARE RUNNING AT FULL SPEED

H   **H**

50 YARD LINE

30 YARD LINE

GOAL LINE

C (COACH)

Figure 38

Half-Moon Drill

We line seven or eight linebackers up in a half-moon with one player two to three yards in front of the half-moon. This is the man with whom we are concerned. His feet must be parallel, knees bent, hips lowered, shoulders forward, and arms loose. The coach or passer looks at one of the men in the half-moon circle, then throws the ball directly to him. The linebacker in front of the group reacts to the passer's eyes first, then the ball. When the passer looks at a particular player in the half-moon

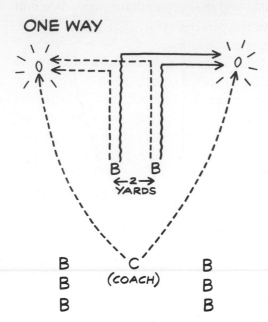

ONE WAY

B
B
B

C
(COACH)

B
B
B

←2→
YARDS

B   B

O   O

Figure 39

circle, the defender must move quickly and align himself between the player and passer, before the ball is thrown.

We teach our linebackers to watch the passer's eyes. Most passers throw in the same direction in which they are looking. Since linebackers are close enough to see the passer's eyes, we believe in exploiting this advantage.

At the outset of the drill we control the situation. The passer looks from one man to another without throwing the ball. Then he looks and throws the ball and the isolated defender throws it back quickly. The passer gradually builds up to

Drills in Pass Defense

where he looks and throws simultaneously. We find that the isolated player's agility, quickness, and reaction increase perceptibly.

After this drill has been used for some time and the isolated player's confidence has been built up by success (which is accomplished by having the individual defender concentrate on watching the passer's eyes first and the ball second), the passer looks at one man in the half-moon circle and throws softly away from the individual defender to another man. At this point we stress watching the passer's eyes, then going for the football.

We have found that this drill gives us many good things aside from increased agility, quickness, and quick reactions by the linebackers. During the drill the defenders get the opportunity to catch the football which is so very important on pass defense. It also is a good conditioner and it is fun, since it is a game. (See *Figure 40.*)

One-on-One Drill

This is a one-on-one drill where the receiver is limited to four basic pass patterns. We realize the defensive man is at a disadvantage but we impress upon him that once he learns to cover a man in this drill consistently, he can do it successfully in a game.

We make the drill competitive by having two groups going simultaneously. One quarterback and center will throw to the left ends, another quarterbacker and center will throw to the right ends. We play one side against the other by keeping count of the number of Jerichoes and completions. Also, we have the number one halfbacks competing against the number two halfbacks, and so forth.

HALF MOON

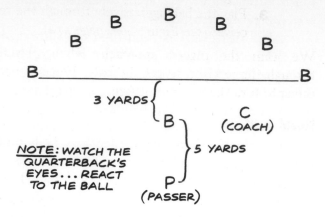

Figure 40

The receivers run the following pass patterns:

1. Hook
2. Square-out
3. Square-in
4. Deep

Once the defenders have covered these patterns, then the offensive men advance to the square-out with the take-off pattern, then the hook-and-go pattern.

In the first phase of this drill, the defender covers the pass cuts without having the ball thrown. Next we combine getting coverage with playing the ball. Later we emphasize getting the Jericho. The following fundamentals are stressed in this drill:

1. The defender must maintain proper position on the receiver.

Drills in Pass Defense

2. The defender cannot allow the receiver to get closer than three yards from him.

3. Play the ball aggressively through the receiver (see *Figure 40a, page 214*).

We want the rugged approach, when playing through the receiver, to get the ball. Force the receiver to turn the ball loose (*Figure 41, page 215*).

Shield Drill

Our shield drill is used for teaching body position. One pass defender holds a shield with seven or eight defensive men lined up five yards away from the shield at various angles. The coach stands eight yards from the shield. When the coach looks at the shield, one of the defensive backs runs toward it. The coach throws the ball and the defender makes the Jericho with both hands, all the while getting and maintaining good body position on the shield. It is important that the defender turn the side of his body into the shield while making the Jericho. He gets both hands on the football regardless of the angle at which he comes into the shield.

Most pass defenders when going for the football with an opponent in the immediate area will go in with their body unprotected and will be satisfied with merely knocking the ball to the ground. Pass defenders who follow this procedure are exposing themselves to injury and will never get the Jericho. This drill is very worthwhile because it teaches the defenders good body position and also provides them with an opportunity to get a Jericho (see *Figure 42*).

Dogfight Drill

We use this drill to teach the defensive man to play through the receiver in an aggressive manner.

Figure 40a: Play the ball aggressively through the receiver.

ONE ON ONE

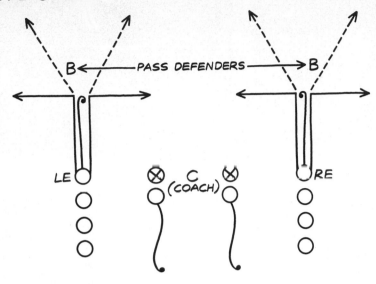

Figure 41

The defensive man lines up in his correct position, depending upon the particular position he plays. The receiver goes downfield and always runs a square-out pattern. The coach throws the ball where the defensive man must play through the receiver to break up the pass. The coach overthrows and underthrows the receiver to see whether the defensive man is watching the passer and playing the ball—not the receiver.

Playing through a receiver does not come naturally to a defensive back. We must work on this maneuver just as we do on any fundamental of pass defense. This drill is a particular favorite of

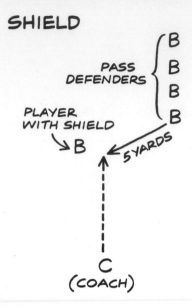

SHIELD

PASS DEFENDERS

B
B
B
B

PLAYER WITH SHIELD

B

5 YARDS

C
(COACH)

Figure 42

ours—because it teaches the pass defender to play the receiver while keeping his vision on the passer until the ball is thrown, then reacting to the ball and playing through the receiver to get the Jericho (see *Figure 43*).

Stance Drill

The stance drill is used in reviewing and correcting the pass defender's stance. All the players involved in pass defense are lined up in the three-deep (special) secondary alignment. On the command, "ready," each man assumes the correct foot position that the specific alignment calls for. After checking the correct foot position the command, "set" is given, and every defender assumes the

Drills in Pass Defense

DOGFIGHT

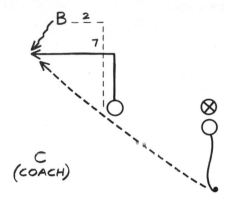

Figure 43

proper stance. This includes bending the knees,
dropping the hips, moving the shoulders forward,
with the arms hanging loose. Now they must be
prepared to react.

When the three-deep alignment has been
checked out we repeat the drill with the pass defenders lined up in a four-deep (box) secondary
alignment. This drill is used periodically to check
the pass defender's stance (see Figure 44, page 218).

Linebacker Post Drill

This is used primarily as a linebacker drill. We
train linebackers to watch the passer's eyes and
react to them. We put two large dummies as posts
10 yards from the line of scrimmage and 10 yards

STANCE

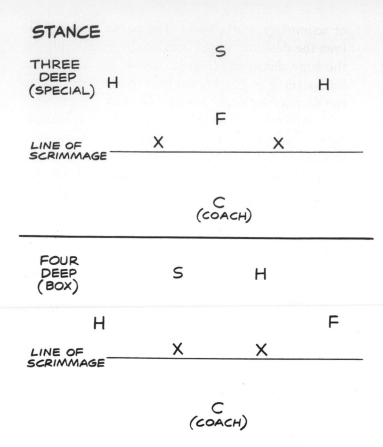

THREE DEEP (SPECIAL)

S

H   H

F

LINE OF SCRIMMAGE ———— X   X ————

C
(COACH)

FOUR DEEP (BOX)

S   H

H   F

LINE OF SCRIMMAGE ———— X   X ————

C
(COACH)

Figure 44

apart. The linebacker stations himself eight yards in front of the bags and midway between them. The other linebackers are in a line beside the coach. We start by having the bags at 10 yards, then as the linebackers learn to go farther for the ball we spread the bags farther apart. The coach drops back to the pocket as the linebacker, two yards away from line

Drills in Pass Defense

of scrimmage, starts back. The passer (coach) allows the defender to get back to the same depth as the large dummies—then he throws the ball. The linebacker is to Jericho the ball. As he gets better, the distance he must go to get the ball is increased.

When the linebacker gets to his hook spot, have him square up, keeping his arms loose, feet moving and squarely underneath him, so he can jump and get maximum height. All the while he must keep his eyes focused on the passer's eyes (see Figure 45).

Stretch Drill

The mechanical part of increasing the distance the pass defender can go to Jericho the pass is acquired and improved by having the defender stand 10 yards to 15 yards from the passer and having the

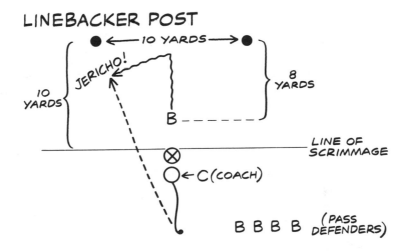

Figure 45

Drills in Pass Defense

passer throw the ball from five to 10 yards to either side of, or behind, the defender. Very soon the defender learns that he can judge accurately where the ball is going and get there to make the Jericho. He soon learns to get the "jump" on the ball just as a good outfielder does in baseball.

Later in the drill have the passer fake a pass in one direction and throw in another. By doing this we teach the difference between the fake throw and the actual throw. On the fake the passer uses a short pumping action with his arm. When he actually throws the ball his arm will follow a complete arc. There is a very definite difference (see *Figure 46*).

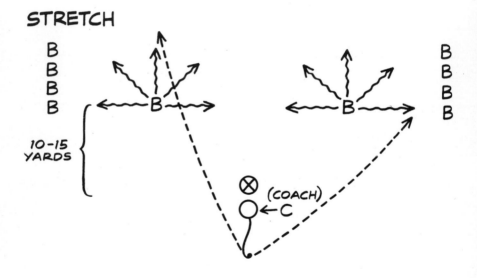

Figure 46

Drills in Pass Defense

In this drill we stress the fundamentals of getting a Jericho, which are:

1. Fly to the ball once it is thrown.
2. Go through the man to get the ball.
3. Look the ball into the hands.
4. Catch the ball at its highest point.
5. Put the ball away.
6. Dig hard for three steps and go for a touchdown.

Index

Personnel placement, 104-06
  in 4-deep pass defense coverage, 131-32
  player's skills and, 104-05
Philosophy of multiple defense, 31-32
Pihos, Pete, 95
Players, sense of pride required of, 43-44
Playing field, as classroom, 168
Playing positions, stances proper to, 85-86
Position on pass receiver, 86
Practice (*see also* Drills):
  distribution of time allotted for, 165
  group work, 171-73
  individual, on pass defense patterns,
    168-69
  multiple defense, 40, 42
  objectives of, 167
  organization of, 180-86
  pass defense, changing purposes of, 177
  2-man pass defense patterns, 169-71
Pre-determine *defined*, 91-92
Psychological warfare, pass defense as,
  76-80
Punt situation, the deceptively "obvious,"
  60

Q

Quarterback, responsibilities of the, 87

R

Reaction to offensive action, 95, 124ff
Responsibilities, division of, 97
Rule:
  cardinal, of pass defense, 100
  the "solid," 115
  six-yard sideline, 86
Running game, 4-deep defenses against,
  158ff
Runs, deep secondary reaction to, 124ff

S

Safetyman:
  keying from call by, 113
  pass coverage by, 147-48

Safetyman (*cont.*)
  role of in calling adjustments, 106-07
Scrimmage line, tackles made at, 95, 96
Signal caller, role of in multiple defense,
  38-39
Six-yard sideline rule, 86
Skill:
  development of group and individual,
    177
  pass defense, 47-48
  player's, and placement, 104-05
Solid formation, pass coverage against,
  114-16
"Solid rule," the, 115
Speranza, Bill, 62
Stance:
  as determined by alignments, 84-87
  footwork drills for, 191-97, 216-17
  playing position and, 85, 106
Star-gazing *defined*, 93-94
"Stay-honest" defense precept, 94-95
Strength, defensive, pre-determination of,
  93
Symbols, use of, 76-80

T

Tackles made at scrimmage line, 95, 96
Tackles, pass defense role of, 50, 51-52
Tackling in pass defense, 50
Talking it up (*see also* Verbal communica-
  tion), 90-91, 99-100
Techniques, drill as perfector of, 189
Temerario, "Tim," 52

Y

Yaksick, Bob, 96
Yardage gained as measure of good pass
  defense, 71

Z

Zone, pass defense coverage, 55-57
  types of, 85, 86
  combined with man-for-man, 58-59